MOATS

Theory of Life

MOATS

Theory of Life

ARTHUR MOATS

with Tisha Sledd

Interior design and typeset by Bookmasters
Cover Design by Vanessa Workoff
Cover Photography by Matt Dayak

Published by:
Leadership League
P.O. Box 828
Mckees Rocks, PA 15136

ISBN: 978-1-7333186-1-7
Library of Congress Control Number: 2019952461

Printed in the United States of America.

For my wife, Shonda, and children, Kaylor, Ava, and Grey. Y'all are my heart and what I am truly most proud of in my life.

Table of Contents

About the Author

From the inner city of Norfolk, Virginia, to a starting position in the NFL, Arthur Moats has lived an incredible life full of twists and turns. His enthusiasm and exuberance for getting the most out of life is contagious to those around him. Fans began cheering his name because of his reputation for being a hard-hitting linebacker. When they began chanting "Don't Cross the Moats," Arthur knew he had found his tribe.

Moats is also known for his philanthropic works. Two different NFL teams have honored him with the Walter Payton Man of the Year award for his excellence on and off the field. Moats has donated a huge percentage of his earnings to various charities and loves to inspire others to become all they were created to be.

Moats retired from the NFL in 2019. He is now a sportscaster for the Pittsburgh Steelers and hosts his own podcast, *The Arthur Moats Experience with Deke*, on iTunes. He lives with his wife Shonda and their three children in Pittsburgh.

Acknowledgments

I have to start by thanking my amazing wife, Shonda, for giving me the confidence and support to embark on this journey of writing a book. The countless hours you spent proofreading, inspiring me with ideas, challenging me to make something special, along with taking care of the children during the writing process was phenomenal, to say the least! I truly couldn't have done this without you. Thank you for everything, my love.

Kaylor aka "KK," Ava aka "Gizmo," Grey aka "G-Money," and Biggie aka "The Big Dog," I want to thank you all for being you! The countless laughs and more serious moments we've shared to this point have been pivotal in my writing of this book. I drew on all four of you wild children for inspiration. I truly hope this book brings smiles to your faces and encourages you as y'all progress through life. Always remember: Daddy loves each of you and Y'ALL ARE ALL MY FAVORITE!

The Original Moats Crew—Arthur Jr. (daddy), Rosalind (mommy), Chrissy aka "My Ace" (sister), and Kelvin aka "K-Rock" (brother)—it's truly been an amazing ride! From growing up together in the "757," and maneuvering through all the twists and turns associated with that, to where we all are now in life. I couldn't have asked for a better family! The life lessons I've learned from each one of you has been major in the development of who I am today. Without y'all there is no me, and I truly appreciate and cherish every moment that we've shared and what moments we will share in the future. I love you!

Uncle Darryl (Uncle D), thanks for always listening and helping me understand the game of football and how to play it the right way. I couldn't have made it this far without you. You are a walking inspiration and a display of what true courage is. Keep pressing on no matter what. Keep being the great man that you are.

Chery (my West Coast mom), it's been a blast ever since your amazing daughter came into my life. From our pregame texts to the competition for who's going to pay for dinner, I appreciate you and everything you've done for me. Your perspective and conversations with me helped in this process more than you know. Also, thank you for sharing your superhero reading skills—proofreading the book and helping me make it perfect. I really appreciate you! Power to the people!

To my team over at Leadership League, I can't thank y'all enough for the countless hours, meetings, and emails that went into making this process a dream come true! Scott Z., Damian, Tisha, and Vanessa, y'all made this process enjoyable for me and challenged me in the right areas. I appreciate y'all not letting me settle for good in this project. Instead, you pushed me until I made something I would be proud of for years to come. I definitely look forward to our next project together because this is only the beginning!

Mr. Arthur J. Rooney II, Coach Mike Tomlin, the entire Pittsburgh Steelers organization, and Steelers Nation, thank you for helping me become the man I am today. I learned so much from my time with this organization. From the opportunity to sign as a free agent to you guys honoring your word and giving me a contract extension, y'all truly changed me and my family's life. Thank you for welcoming us with open arms and embracing us as one of your own! #HereWeGo

To my Buffalo Bills family and Bills Mafia, I will always have a special place in my heart for y'all! This is where it all started for me.

Y'all took a chance on a kid from JMU and helped him achieve his childhood dream of being a football player in the NFL. Y'all provided me with the foundation I needed to accomplish my goals both on and off the field. Thanks for everything and let's go Buffalo!

J-M-U Dukessssss! To the amazing people at James Madison University, thank you for providing me with a top-tier education, helping me advance my playing career, and introducing me to my wife. Y'all helped in so many ways that I don't feel I will ever be able to repay it. I couldn't ask to have attended a better university. I'll forever cherish the relationships, life lessons, and memories I acquired during my time there! Go Dukes!

Owen, Brian, and Monty you have each impacted my life in ways I could never have imagined. Your courage, drive, and desire to be great continues to inspire me to this day. I've learned very vital lessons from each of you that help me grow daily. I'm excited to see where you guys go in life and the great things y'all will continue to accomplish. Keep being great in all you do and know I'm always proud of you!

To the "757," thank you for the life lessons you taught me. Every bump, bruise, smile, and cry was needed to help me to get to where I am today. I appreciate every aspect of you because it educated me on so many levels, and without those lessons, I wouldn't be the man I am. Some of my best and worst memories have come from you, and I wouldn't have it any other way! Shark City and P-Town stand up!

I have to give a big thank-you to the United States Marine Corps. Without you guys teaching my father the qualities and life lessons he learned, I would never have been able to learn the things I needed. Because of you, I have the mental fortitude to smile and keep going forward through it all. Thank you for keeping this amazing country safe and as always, *SEMPER FI!*

And finally, I definitely have to thank the Man above for never leaving me nor forsaking me throughout my life. I am grateful to You for giving me this platform to positively impact lives! Through You, I've been able to achieve and overcome things I would've never imagined! Thank You!

Introduction

First and Ten

It's not whether you get knocked down, it's whether you get up.
—Vince Lombardi

THE NEXT STEP

My senior year of playing college football was going great. I was looking forward to the next step of my journey. I was going to play in the NFL! I was twenty-two, and life was looking mighty fine from my end. My name was moving up on the draft board. Nothing was going to come between me and my dream.

I had returned from the NFL combine. A couple of my teammates and I were back at James Madison University (JMU), and we had just finished a workout. ESPN was on the TV in the background, but we were just messing around having a good time, not really paying attention to the TV.

But then we heard Mel Kiper, an NFL draft guru who had been doing this for over 20 years, talking about a player who impressed him. Kiper said, "Long arms, a little bit undersized, but very muscular, compact figure, great first step, double-digit sacks two years in a row. He led the nation his senior year in tackles for a loss. He's a highly productive player, and he's got a great motor …" The list just kept getting longer!

As I was listening, I was thinking, *Dude, whoever he is talking about is some phenomenal guy.*

Kiper kept going, "This guy is going to be an absolute steal. Whatever team gets him is going to love him. He is going to go … I can see him as high as the third round but at worst case fifth round. Anything after the fifth round would be absolutely insane that he would be on the board that long." *Geez! Who is this guy talking about?*

We started paying more attention to Kiper as he talked about this guy, and then he transitioned to a highlight tape, and who was on the highlight tape?

Me!

Kiper was talking about me! My guys and I started jumping around like little schoolgirls, wearing our compression shorts and socks, and they just kept saying, "Dude! Mel Kiper is talking about you on ESPN!" Because I went to such a small school, I never dreamed of being on ESPN. Now I was watching an entire segment on me and ESPN was showing my highlight film.

I remember watching at that moment and feeling like *Holy cow! This is insane!* Kiper had been talking about me. It was the ultimate validation. It was a well-known fact that if Mel Kiper or Todd Mc-Shay said you were going to get drafted, you were more than likely going to be drafted. *Crazy feeling, man!*

My family and I were extremely excited. I was about to live out my dream. It was getting closer and closer each day, and my excitement and expectations were building. Kiper actually called me a steal!

DRAFT DAY

So draft day arrived, and we decided to go to Buffalo Wild Wings and watch the first round. No phone call from any of the NFL teams on that first day, but that's okay. I had already been told I would be taken in the third round "at best" and the fifth round "at worst." *Mel Kiper said so!*

Day two rolls around, and we went to my uncle's house to have a nice little NFL draft party. At the end of the round, still no calls, but that's fine. I was chill about it all. *No worries, it's all good.* But I made sure all my devices were charged. I made sure my mother's cell phone had service, and she was all charged up as well. You have to give them two numbers so they can be sure to contact you.

The third round started, and then I got an email from the Kansas City Chiefs. The scout was making sure he had the correct information because I was still on their board. I thought to myself, *Cool. I can handle being a Kansas City Chief. I can smell that BBQ from here!* But the third round went by, and there wasn't anything but crickets from my phone. I checked the battery. I made sure I had a signal. It's all good. Except for the fact that it wasn't ringing. At this point, I was getting a little antsy.

Later in the third round, the San Francisco 49ers were on the clock. I began thinking about my trip out to San Fran and how they flew me out there. *It was nice!* I remembered how well I clicked with Coach Singletary. *It was really nice,* I thought. He had even called my high school coach, my mother, AND my father to see what kind of guy I was and if I could play linebacker. I thought to myself, *It's about to happen! They absolutely have to pick me, right? It makes perfect sense. They need a linebacker. I am a linebacker. I am a high trade guy at the time. It is going to be a perfect fit.* And then my nice little dream shattered.

The 49ers chose a linebacker out of Penn State, NaVorro Bowman. They announced it on the TV, and I'm shaking my head. *What? NaVorro Bowman? Are they serious?* (Hindsight being 20/20 it was a great pick for them! He's a future Hall of Famer for sure!)

Even after this shot to my ego, I kept my hopes up. *It's okay. I'm still in this.* But what happened next caused me to completely lose my mind.

Now it's time for the fifth round, and there are camera crews at my house. It's a big deal for a guy from a little town to go to the NFL. Now the pressure is on. I needed to maintain my cool. As the fifth round started, no one seemed to be taking linebackers. The Tampa Bay Buccaneers actually took a punter *(a punter?)* from Virginia Tech in the fifth round … before me! It physically hurt my heart that a punter got taken before me. Now I know that punters are people too. I've got nothing against them. But I'm a baller! Or at least I thought I was.

On the inside, I was really losing it. My family was trying to support me by saying, "Hey man, we're sorry for what you're going through. We understand." But they didn't. The NFL is not like a regular job. It's not like you can take your résumé to different franchises and try again. That was something I felt no one could relate to. And at this point, I didn't even want to watch the draft anymore. I immediately went to the worst-case scenario: *Football is over. I'm never going to play again.* I went upstairs to throw my little pity party. But it's cool because I did it with dignity in another room. I didn't let anybody else see me, at least that's what I told myself.

I couldn't let my family and the camera crews see me fall apart with all the doubt and confusion swirling around me. Arrows of lies start coming toward my mind. *I am a public failure. I'm a failure in life. School doesn't matter. I can't go to Canada because it would be an embarrassment. They took a punter before me! What am I going to do with my life now?*

And then the phone rang. *Thank you, Jesus!*

The sixth round had started, and the New York Giants were calling me. Their scout explained to me that they were going to trade up in order to pick me in this round. "We are happy you're still available. We love what you do, and we think you could be a great player, a great asset to us." Now I am excited! I'm going to New York City!

NOT A LOSER

I started walking downstairs to tell my family that now we had some action! I was going to tell them that everything was all right and I was going to be picked later in the round. *It was all good!*

Then the phone rang again!

It was the Atlanta Falcons. They said, "We don't pick this round, but we're going to trade back in so we can pick you!" *What? Now I'm gonna be an Atlanta Falcon?*

My walk back down the stairs turned into an all-out sprint! This whole time the Buffalo Bills have been on the clock. They had been trying to get ahold of me, but I'd been tied up on the phone, so they called my mother. They were all excited for me. When I got downstairs I announced with no small amount of enthusiasm that I was either going to play for the New York Giants or the Atlanta Falcons. But they told me no! You're going to be a Buffalo Bill because they are on the clock and they are picking you right now!

I hung up on the Falcons and grabbed the phone from my mom and on the other end is Buddy Nix, general manager at the time for the Buffalo Bills. He said, "You're going to be a Buffalo Bill. Welcome to the family." *Ha! Take that punter!*

I remember walking to the TV and watching my name get called. I was just overcome with emotion. I remember falling on the floor, my cousins and everyone going crazy! It was one of the best feelings I have ever experienced. Honestly, it was one of the best days of my life. The Buffalo Bills gave me an opportunity to live out my dream. They allowed me to experience the fulfillment of my desires after all the years of hard work and sacrifice.

It was a mountaintop experience for sure! But as wonderful as this mountaintop was … there was a valley around the corner.

THE FIRST TRAINING CAMP

Rookie season training camp was the worst one ever! I was on the bottom of the pile. The odds were stacked against me. Along with not having a choice of what team you play for, you also don't get to choose what position you're going to play. So, my whole career, from high school through college, I played defensive end. And the Buffalo Bills decided to move me to inside linebacker. The difference in positions was night and day. Inside linebacker is a completely different outlook, with completely different responsibilities.

During the preseason, I got a ton of plays because other people were getting injured, and it had given me an opportunity to play, but the change in position was killing me. I couldn't seem to pull it together. They would tell me to go in the B gap, and I went in the A gap, or they would tell me to drop in coverage, and I would rush the quarterback. These were all the things that I was messing up on. If there had been a stat for leading the league in mental errors, I definitely broke that record. And this was all during that first training camp, that first preseason. *It was killing me.*

It was the first time I've ever thought I wasn't good enough. I was going to get cut or in this case, fired because it's the NFL and that's how they roll.

To my surprise, one of the radio analysts said something like, "Don't Cross the Moats!" He had seen me making some good plays and was impressed by what he saw on the field. But what he didn't know was that I was not running the plays I'd been given. I was using my instincts instead. There were plenty of times that I was supposed to be running and not really covering a guy. Or the times I followed the ball instead of sticking with my assignment.

I had plenty of conversations with my parents on the phone during training camp that I should not rent an apartment. I felt my time in the NFL would be short. I just could not stop making mental mistakes. My dad, a former marine, said to me, "This is a process. And whatever happens through this adversity you are going to come out of it better. You are built to be successful." He kept reassuring me, "No matter how bad it looks right now, no matter how bleak it might seem, you are going to come through this. You are going to have a positive impact. You are going to be a success. SEMPER FI!"

I decided to believe my dad. I took one day at a time, one game at a time, one play at a time, and eventually, it led me to have a successful first year.

At the end of my first preseason, I had focused so much on turning my fear into hustle that I ended up leading the whole NFL in tackles that preseason. I wasn't doing anything special—I was just out there, running around hitting people, trying to look like I knew what I was doing. *Ha!*

DON'T CROSS THE MOATS

Fast-forward to Week 13 of the regular season. I was still just a rookie. I was playing a little on special teams with a sprinkling on defense, but I was young. It was the Minnesota Vikings game. I'm a huge Brett Favre fan! *Huge!*

Favre had played in the NFL for twenty years, which was crazy in itself! Not only that, but he started for a consecutive twenty years! He's played 297 games and started every single one of them. He never missed a game. He'd been sacked and hit by numerous Hall of Famers. Guys like Michael Strahan, Brian Urlacher, and Julius Peppers had their opportunity to take Favre down!

My first play in, Favre started scrambling out of the pocket. I was able to shed my blocker, started pursuing him from the backside. It was exactly like I had practiced all week leading up to the game. I was able to connect with him in a manner that every pass rusher dreams about. It was the perfect blindside hit. The ball flew from his hand after the hit, and it ended up being intercepted, which was a huge part of the game. But after the play, I got up, and Favre didn't. He was hurt.

Not just hurt a little, but my tackle actually caused him to not start the next game. His starting streak was ended. Then, all of a sudden, it became a legendary play.

Summed up best by Buffalo Rumblings blog: "Brett Favre started 297 consecutive games at quarterback from 1992 through 2010. Then he played against Arthur Moats, an unassuming rookie sixth-round pick out of James Madison, and one big hit ended arguably the best consecutive games played streak in the history of sports."[1]

My friends on the team started calling me "Legend Killer" and "Streak Ender." And then the phrase "Don't Cross the Moats" was getting new traction. It actually blew up from there. It took on a new life because it was now heard from a national standpoint. The video was played over and over. And people all over were saying:

"Don't Cross the Moats!"

THE NEXT CHAPTER OF LIFE

After nine years in the NFL, I can say that I've been so blessed to experience the ups and downs of this journey. I've learned so much through the life I've been given and worked for. Accomplishing my dreams and experiencing the thrill of reaching my goals has inspired me to encourage others to go after their dreams.

There is nothing quite like inspiring greatness in others. It's something I have endeavored to do my entire life. From playing drums in my parents' church as a child to competing as an NFL linebacker in front of millions of people, my focus has been to lead others to their highest, most impactful selves.

I've lived an incredible life with so many opportunities. But like many others, my journey has been filled with ups and downs, zigs, and zags. My personal failures and the eventual overcoming of those failures has given me a passion for helping others with their journey.

We've all been given valleys to climb out of, mountains to conquer, and relationships to grow through as we walk through this biggest, most important game called life. I want to share a little of my story with you hoping that you might find encouragement and inspiration to keep climbing, keep surviving, and keep pressing into relationships with those around you.

I've found that when we share what we have learned through our losses and our victories, we help each other stand a little taller, spark a little more courage, and spread hope to give the game of life one more try.

This book I've written is not meant to be an autobiography. That is not my aim. I'm not trying to give you an in-depth play-by-play of my life in the pages ahead. I'll save that for down the road somewhere. Right now, at this time in my life, I want to be a proactive inspirer. I want to tell a few of my stories with one purpose in mind: To open people up to the greatness that resides in them.

I've organized my inspirational thoughts in a way that is near and dear to my heart. I'll share my pain and my gains. I'll share the wisdom from my heartache and the lessons from my victories. I hope you will take this journey with me as I open up my heart and share with you the M.O.A.T.S. Theory of Life.

M.O.A.T.S. Theory of Life

THE STATUS QUO

Life. The most important of all gifts. Seeing my children born was one of the greatest experiences of my life. That precious gift, that bundle of potential was put into my hands to love and protect. What a feeling to watch a baby take its first breath. I'll never forget it as long as I live.

There is so much promise in that baby. So many possibilities wrapped up in the life of a child. It was as though I came alive again. Every breath my children took was an extension of me. My hopes and dreams had a new meaning. Whatever I achieved in my life, was a floor they could now stand on. My ceiling was their floor.

I found a new desire to reach higher. I found a passion to get the junk out of my soul. I wanted to fully live out my dreams and then watch them live out theirs.

But if I was going to give them a sturdy platform to launch from, I had some work to do. I needed to reawaken my purpose. I needed to find my God-given identity and pour everything I could into it. I needed for the real Arthur Moats to come alive.

We all have a purpose written into our DNA. There are things each of us have been put here on earth to achieve. Every person is a part of a bigger puzzle. We are teachers, leaders, encouragers, servants, preachers, justice seekers, protectors, entertainers, and healers. Every person's purpose fits into someone else's dream. Part of our issue is that we've been disconnected from our dreams, and our purpose has been lost in the storms of life. We got distracted by fear. We lost sight of our original goals. Life got monotonous, and like a wave carrying away Wilson from Tom Hanks in *Castaway,* we watched our dream get further and further away. And we felt helpless to do anything about it.

I had gotten carried away by the meaningless parts of life. The hollow part for me was trying to make my life look great from the outside. Even though I was in the NFL and it looked like I was living the dream, inwardly I was wasting away because I got disconnected from my dreams.

It turns out that my dream wasn't dead. It just needed to be watered.

Having my children caused me to face the truth that life is a precious gift. If I was going to give them everything they needed to succeed, I needed to become everything I was called to be. I needed to finish my race, so they could finish theirs. Something had to change in me. Something had to awaken what had been lulled to sleep. My purpose and my dreams needed a resurrection.

How about you? Are you truly living?

Are you fully inhabiting your purpose and your dreams? Or have they been lulled to sleep like mine were?

I'm trying to make you a little uncomfortable. I want my words to possibly hurt you a little. Because I want to awaken what is in you. I want to hold up a mirror to your life right now and ask if you like what you see? Are you where you're supposed to be? Are you doing the things you're called to do? Are you working to improve your life and the life of your family?

Or have you been stuck in a rut?

I want this book to be a whisper in your ear and a wake-up call to your conscience. I want you to become dissatisfied with the status quo. In football, when a coach wanted to break up the status quo we'd have to start doing different drills. If we fell into a rut, the coach would have to use a different tactic to get our eyes on the prize again.

Like Henry Ford said, "If you always do what you've always done, you'll always get what you've always got." If your dreams and purpose seem like they are dead or asleep, you've got to figure out a way to bring them back to life. Because if you don't change the status quo, you will simply get more status quo.

PRISONS OF THE MIND

Are you in a prison in your mind? Have you said to yourself, "It's too late for me?" Have you bought into the lie that your circumstances won't allow you to fulfill your purpose and dreams? This is where I want to shoot my arrow. I want to aim for the complacency and doubt in your mind. I want to cause you to take a good look at your life and to open your mind to the fact that you may be in a mind prison voluntarily.

Maybe the "status quo prison" feels hopeless. Maybe you've decided that there is simply no way forward. But I want to challenge that mind-set. Who said you had to stay there? Who said that you could only achieve your purpose and dreams to a certain level? Those are lies sent by the enemy of our souls. Fear is coming after you to steal your life. But I've come to tell you, this status quo prison is actually made of tiny little sticks. It's easy to overcome. You just have to stand up and become curious again.

The quickest way out of the status quo prison is to become curious. Begin to be curious about what might be ahead for you. Be curious about your purpose. Why did God create you? Who might need what only you have to give? What is your *why*? Every single person has a *why*. There's a part for everyone to play in this game of life. The puzzle fits together as we each play our part.

I need what you have. You need what I have. The next generation will need our children. It will be important for them to live out their purposes and their dreams. But first, we must complete what we have been put here to complete.

There are no excuses. Not enough money, not enough support, not enough time—those are all cop-outs! They are all lies that come from fear. I want to get to the end of my life and know that I left it all on the field. I played every play of the game. I left nothing undone.

I want to awaken your mind to the fact that the game isn't over and we gotta start playing with a little more passion. We gotta understand that there is a generation that comes after us. They are counting on us to prepare the way for them. We do this by finishing our race. We prepare the way for the next generation by completing our purposes. We become an example of how to truly live life.

I've not only come to challenge you to live life with a little more passion. I also want to share my theory about how to take steps toward your purpose. I know that many would be surprised to find that playing in the NFL was never my purpose. While it was an amazing experience to reach this goal of mine, and it would seem like the ultimate storyline, it wasn't the fulfillment I had been looking for.

I had to go on a journey to figure out my *why.*

While I share my journey with you, I hope to inspire you with courage. It's okay to question why you feel stuck. It's okay to question the status quo. There is a path to fulfilling your purpose. Your dreams aren't dead. They just need to be watered.

This theory of mine is just that—a theory. It's my belief, my policy, my suggested procedure to find your *why* and begin to live it out loud. I want to share with you what ultimately shined a light on my purpose and how I started my journey out of the status quo prison.

My theory was born out of my pain. It was formed as I traveled through the mountains and valleys that came my way. We will all have peaks and valleys to overcome in life, but sharing what we learn through them can be a priceless gift we can give to those we walk beside.

I'm going to share with you the importance of making happiness a priority and how openness yields strength. I want to motivate you to actively inspire others. I want to help you turn your fear into focus and to help you spread your inner love.

These are a few of my theories of life.

HAPPINESS A PRIORITY

Happiness cannot be traveled to, owned, earned, worn, or consumed.
Happiness is the spiritual experience of living every minute, with love, grace, and gratitude.

—Denis Waitley

FALLING INTO ROUTINE

It's so easy to get caught up in the day-in and day-out routine. We go to work. We help the kids with homework. We eat dinner, sleep, wake up, and do it all over again. When we fall into that routine, we easily forget what happiness truly feels like. We try to find comfort in our situation by saying things like:

"Everything is fine."
"I'm grinding for my family."
"I'm a go-getter!"
"This is real life."

We use clichés like this to justify our lack of happiness and the true meaning of life, which is to LIVE!

If you find yourself using clichés, you probably better look in the mirror and ask the hard question: Have you been swallowed up by the routine instead of truly living life?

As we look at ourselves in the mirror, we gotta ask the hard questions. Are we happy? Or are we wearing a mask and pretending that we are. I'm telling you, there are a lot of us out here who are really good pretenders. We know how to make that mask work for everyone around us. The mask of "Good Dad" hides our insecurity or fear of failing as a parent. The mask of "Provider" hides our tiredness and puffs up our weary ego. The mask of "Attentive Husband" hides the wounds that need to be addressed because we have to be the strong one.

Some of us have fallen so far into the routine and hidden behind the masks that we've forgotten what happiness really looks like.

Well, I'm gonna tell you something that might sound strange at first, but go with me. The road to happiness starts by figuring out what makes your own soul light up. What electrifies you as a person? What is it that turns on the light inside of you and starts pumping those endorphins of happiness? The first step toward happiness is focusing on you.

It might seem counterintuitive because we've been programmed with thinking everyone else in your life must be happy before you can be happy. We've been told that our sole focus in life is making sure everyone else is happy while constantly putting our feelings in the next time slot. But if you constantly put everyone else first and never pay attention to the needs of your own soul, you will never be able to experience happiness.

I can tell you that for certain because I lived that way for a long time, and it honestly was eating me alive from the inside out like a disease. From the surface, I looked happy, but truthfully, I was wearing masks to hide what was really going on. I had to be the go-getter who didn't allow my family or myself to fail. I understood sacrifices were necessary to reach success, and I believed the lie that my happiness was just a price I would have to pay or as I would tell my extra-macho self, "My happiness is a casualty of war, and once this battle is won I'll rest upon my throne and marvel at my accomplishments."

It sounds good and self-sacrificing, like something you would hear in a war movie where the underdog loses everything to reach greatness. The only problem is: *That's not LIVING!*

For me to reach true happiness and live a life with meaning and purpose, I had to learn to prioritize myself. What were the things in this world that brought me to life? What was it that fed my soul? I truly had no idea. I had forgotten because the routine of life had swallowed me whole. I began taking steps toward putting my own needs first sometimes. The first step consisted of figuring out what truly brought me happiness and pleasure.

MEMORY LANE

I thought back to some of my happiest moments with my family. But I began to feel swallowed up again in false responsibility. I immediately felt the "everyone else has to come first" lie.

So, I started thinking about my success as a football player before playing professionally, and I had some really fond memories! I thought about the time I had 3.5 sacks in a playoff game on ESPN2. *Man, that was cool!* Or that time I scored my first collegiate touchdown as a true freshman and made the cover of the school paper. *A touchdown, baby!* Or that time we went undefeated in the CAA and won the conference championship. *A truly unbelievable feeling!*

As I walked down memory lane of my collegiate athletic career, none of those memories were leaving me fulfilled.

They were great times and memories that my teammates and I talk about whenever we get together, but it just wasn't giving me the feeling I was searching for. Great memories of success were fun for a moment, but they were momentary and didn't bring a consistent light to my soul. I obviously needed to dig deeper.

I decided to think about my adolescent years, and once again, I found myself going down the Arthur Moats Sports Hall of Fame. Memories of my success at the Virginia High School League Group AAA State Wrestling Tournament where I placed eighth, or that time I had a monstrous dunk against Lake Taylor to complete my double-double, or when I was voted Second Team All-State in football. *Ahh, memory lane is great!* All of these memories were fun and brought a smile to my face, but once again, I still had that feeling of desiring more.

I took it a step further and thought back to when I was around eight years old growing up in Campostella, a lower-income neighborhood in Norfolk, Virginia. I grew up in the church because both of my parents were pastors, and I was the lead drummer, so I was constantly at church. I am not talking just the typical Sunday and Wednesday service. When I say I was constantly at church, I was really constantly at church!

We held a normal Sunday morning service at our church. Then we held two more services at other churches on Sunday afternoon and evening. Monday was the new members class. Tuesday, we had worship rehearsal. Wednesday night was church service. Guess what we did on Thursday, Friday, and Saturday nights? Well, we had church service, of course! Then we were back at it Sunday like I never left! *Ha!*

During that time, I remembered what we did as a church on Saturdays and Sundays. We would go to other low-income neighborhoods in the Norfolk community and deliver loaves of bread for free. We would simply tell people, "Jesus loves you," and that was it.

I remember the looks on these people's faces and the pure joy they would receive from that simple gesture. I also remembered the fear and anxiety I would have going up to these people's homes that I didn't know and praying the whole time that I didn't get shot during the process. They were very rough neighborhoods.

But the people really opened up to us. The love we offered them caused them to open their hearts to us. These people who lived hardened lives and closed themselves off to outsiders melted when we offered them something with no strings attached. They welcomed us into their lives. As I thought back about these random acts of kindness, I realized that it always amazed me that when we offered these small, seemingly insignificant gifts, the people would open their doors to us and we could offer them hope in return.

In reviewing this childhood memory, I found the feeling I was longing for! It was a feeling of pure happiness, and I couldn't get the smile to leave my face after recalling these memories! This is what brought fuel to my soul. It's the feeling in this memory!

I took my time and processed my feelings about these memories. I dug down into my heart to find the root of what it did to my soul. I learned that my innate happiness is driven by bringing joy to others while inspiring hope within them. Once I realized this, I started thinking of other moments where I was able to inspire and bring joy to others, and I instantly became overwhelmed with happiness! I needed to find an outlet where I could help others in need. I needed to find a place where I could make a difference by inspiring others with hope.

Several things fell into place for me. I realized to bring joy to my own soul, I simply needed to find people who needed hope, knock on their door with kindness, and then let my light shine to inspire them with love.

The root of my happiness was not related to success on the field or even in my home. The root of happiness for me was to get outside of my own four walls and inspire others on their path of life. This began to be my purpose.

THE MISSING PIECE

As I began to make my happiness a priority, I started focusing on my community work. It was important for me to make an impact off the field as well as on the field. I wanted to make a difference in whatever city I lived in.

My community work in Buffalo started out with the United Way. Initially, I started out as an intern as a part of my undergraduate responsibilities, just learning the process of community work. At the time, people would ask me why I was juggling volunteering and my education while also playing professional football. But I always felt it was important to get my college degree and continue educating myself, even while being a professional athlete. That way, one wouldn't take away from the other, and all the while would inspire others to do the same.

There was a particular case that broke my heart as my family and I did community work with the Buffalo Red Cross. It was Christmastime, and a local family's house burned down. All the gifts, the Christmas decorations, and the furniture inside their home was gone. My family and I felt called to reach out to this family. It was an opportunity to directly impact people's lives.

Ultimately, even though I knew I was going to feel great from helping the family, it was never about the recognition. It created so much personal joy in me just to have a positive impact on somebody's life when they needed it the most.

As my family and I had a conversation about how we could help, we had an idea to refurnish everything they lost, as well as make sure they had a nice Christmas. But it was so much more than just taking care of the monetary aspect of their needs. We decided to have a meal catered and then join them for a sit-down dinner to fellowship with them.

We were able to surprise the family by bringing dinner to them. My wife and I took our girls, and we told them we had heard about their situation. It would have been easy for us just to cut a check, but we really wanted to be with them to encourage them. We wanted them to understand that it was more than money. It was about the direct person-to-person impact. It's my wholehearted belief that being present for someone when they need help is going to last considerably longer than simply handing out money.

Being able to have that dinner with them and seeing the family's joy were quite uplifting. They were so emotional because they knew no one was forcing us to do this, but it was simply coming from an authentic place in our hearts. We cared about their pain, and we wanted to make a positive impact on them.

I saw this as a win in multiple aspects because not only am I positively impacting their life, it's going to have a direct correlation on my happiness. At the same time, what is that showing my kids? It's showing them the importance of helping out others when you have the opportunity. I love that we are showing them about investing in people at such a young age.

Now they are open in their spirits to give to other charitable initiatives. My daughter loves to help out animals. So, we've given to Animal Friends and various other animal-related organizations. But it all started from this type of event with the family whose house burned down at Christmas. Having a dinner with them and fellowshipping with them led to so much more.

I was able to work even more with the United Way and the Buffalo Red Cross, and it opened the door for me to receive the team's Walter Payton Man of the Year Award. This is an award given to a player on each team that exemplifies excellence both on the field and off the field through their community outreach. It's a huge honor to be recognized for your work in philanthropic endeavors but also your success on the field as well. It's one of the most prestigious community awards you can get in the NFL. Receiving that in Buffalo was a huge deal.

BATMAN

As we moved to Pittsburgh, and I started playing for the Steelers, I had the same concept in my heart. How do we continue to make a difference? What organizations can we get involved with?

We heard about the Ronald McDonald House Charities. Once again, I was really drawn in because of the kids. We learned that so many kids and their families were dealing with extended stays. Some of them were getting transplants or fighting cancer. They were relocating from all over the world to Pittsburgh for medical care. They were able to stay at no cost in the Ronald McDonald House.

There was a family who came all the way from Spain. They had been living in the Ronald McDonald House for three years! They had to leave their home for the sake of their child. Most of the families at the Ronald McDonald House didn't have any extended family nearby. It was just Mom and Dad and their kids. Some of them were losing their jobs because they were not able to go to work. Everything had taken a backseat to the welfare of their child's health.

I remember Owen. At the time he had to use a wheelchair and had to wear a mask because he could not afford to intake any germs. They would have jeopardized his transplant. I remember going there and doing an ice cream social. It was something fun we did with the kids. I loved it because it was all about fellowshipping. I connected right off with Owen because of Batman! He had a Batman phone case, and I had a Batman tattoo.

We just had this connection, and we talked and talked and talked while enjoying our ice cream. I told him how awesome he was. Seeing how motivated Owen was to keep going was an inspiration. He was still upbeat even though he was going through this terrible situation.

He felt the same about me. He said, "Man, you're inspiring me because you're an NFL player, you're a hero, and you're here spending that time with me? You're here doing this for my family and me, and you didn't have to do this."

I got to see him get better and better at the hospital in Pittsburgh. He was released to go back home to Buffalo. I got to see him grow and develop, and now he's in middle school.

His family was able to join us for a game when we played Buffalo. I surprised him with an autographed jersey for his birthday. I loved to do the small things just to inspire him. I was honored to see how this kid who had been wheelchair bound and susceptible to germs grow into a healthy young man competing in sports. We were able to talk about the day we first met and talked about Batman. He appreciated what we were able to do for him and his family. But more so, he appreciated the positive influence I was able to have on him as far as encouraging him to go after his dreams and goals. *It was all because of Batman, baby!*

That all started at the Ronald McDonald House. Once again, I was able to give my family some generational sustenance. I was able to build a foundation of never just doing something once, so it makes you look good. You've gotta build a relationship and then take care of it. Make sure you see them all the way through.

TRUE IMPACT

A few months after that, I thought to myself, *Let's make an impact at James Madison University.* It's my alma mater. I've gotta keep on going with the things that make me happy. Again, not for the accolades—those are just empty praise. But we give to people in order to make a true impact.

I feel like when we talk about the most common forms of community outreach, it's always kids, veterans, and elderly. A lot of times, the collegiate age group or the sixteen- and seventeen-year-olds are getting overlooked.

My family made it a focal point for us to not only target those age groups but make a large impact on those age groups. As we talked about JMU, I wondered, *How can we impact this university and the young adults that go here? How can I, in particular, say thank you to a university that was pivotal in my education, advancing my football career, and helping me find my wife?* That's when we decided to make a very substantial donation to the university that would impact multiple areas we were passionate about.

We felt it was very important to spread our donation over a couple of areas because typically when athletes donate to their colleges, the money is solely sports based. I always prided myself on being more than an athlete, and I felt this was just another opportunity to show that I don't just say that, my actions support it. We decided to designate the funds to the football program, the new convocation center, and to the arts program. We felt these various areas would be very impactful to the university and something that all the students and the city could enjoy.

I'm very passionate about art. I love to draw. I love portraits. I love all these types of things. Along with that, my middle daughter loves to draw and paint as well. My wife and oldest daughter love photography. So, we decided to go ahead and create a scholarship for a student who wanted to major in the arts programs.

We wanted to give scholarships to kids who technically wouldn't come to JMU because of the expense. Normally scholarships for sports are far more generous than scholarships for art. So, we decided to create the Arthur and Shonda Moats Endowed Scholarship for Studio Art. Our goal was to empower students to major in their passion at JMU.

The first recipient of our scholarship is currently going into her junior year at the college. She's in the arts program. We are thrilled to witness how she's flourishing and developing.

I want people to be inspired to give back in thoughtful ways. I want people to understand that it's more than talk. Talk is easy. Actions are harder. But they speak so much louder.

We were able to give JMU $300,000 for the scholarship fund, and it felt awesome! I had people ask me why I donated so much after I had just got my contract with the Steelers. I tell people that I have always had a vision of going back to my college and going back to the inner-city communities and giving back. I want to impact them. It's what makes me happy. I want to leave them better than I found them. I had the platform and the funds, and it was time to go for it!

In a fantastic turn of events, I again received the Walter Payton Man of the Year award, this time as a Steeler. Now instead of being a one-time winner, I became a two-time winner while I played for two different organizations! It was insane from a league standpoint because that does not happen.

Impacting people feeds my soul and makes me happy. I'm not doing it for the applause. I'm doing it to raise other people up.

The applause of men is an empty return on your good deeds. But truly making a difference in the lives of others fills you with purpose and it will not return void.

True happiness ... is not attained through self-gratification, but through fidelity to a worthy purpose.

—Helen Keller

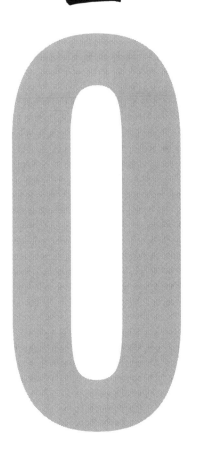

Openness

YIELDS STRENGTH

The strongest love is the love that can demonstrate its fragility.

—Paulo Coelho

MR. MACHO

"Everything is fine!"

It was the favorite tagline of Mr. Macho. Mr. Macho used to be my alter ego. He was incredible. He was powerful. He could handle anything that came his way. His life was always put together, and no matter what circumstances he found himself in, his response to any situation was, "Everything is fine!"

The tagline was always delivered with my signature pearly white smile. I had to make it believable. Because I could not afford for anyone to see the real me. I couldn't let anyone see that I was full of fear and dying on the inside. My alter ego believed that if I really let my wife in, she would reject me. She would be ashamed of me and my fear. So, I built a really good costume to wear. I named him Mr. Macho, and he became a wall between my wife and me.

However, after some time, our little disagreements about my lack of communication and emotions was going to lead to a major blowup. My inability to communicate my feelings led to a disconnect between us. Mr. Macho was bringing pain and suffering to our marriage.

Every time Shonda asked me something, the answer was always, "Everything is fine."

She would ask me, "How was work?"

I would answer, "Fine." And then think, *But I just lost my starting job.*

"How are you getting along with your family?"

"Fine." *But I'm not on speaking terms with my sister, who's my ace boon coon!*

"How's school?"

"Fine." *But these classes are killing me, and I might fail out of the master's program. How embarrassing would that be?*

"How are you feeling?"

"Fine." *But my favorite uncle in the world who never missed my high*

school or college football games is battling cancer for the second time in three years, and

just the thought of losing him is killing me inside.

Mr. Macho would never let me say how I was really feeling. His tagline was his protection. "Everything is fine."

It took us having a serious heart to heart where she expressed her displeasure with my emotions or the lack thereof and how she was becoming tired of the one-sided relationship. It took courage for her to sit me down and essentially give me an ultimatum for me to finally realize, I'm about to lose the most amazing person ever because of my stubbornness and insecurity.

Something had to give. Mr. Macho was leading me down the path to being Mr. Single. I could continue being Mr. Macho, or I could drop the facade and actually open up to my wife. She's the one person I should actually be able to tell everything in a safe judgment-free environment. She's the one person who would love me regardless of how vulnerable I was.

Even though it was extremely tough for me because it was totally out of my comfort zone, I decided to bet it all on red. *My roulette people know what this means.* I had to start opening up about all my feelings and fears.

It was the most uncomfortable, vulnerable, craziest, most awesome feeling EVER! It honestly took our marriage to a totally different level and helped us grow and understand each other more than I could've ever imagined.

I have found that when I am open and authentic with those who are closest to me, I end up gaining strength from that authenticity.

Openness can be an easy thing to say, but a much more difficult task to perform. Openness can be very challenging at times because it goes against our human nature and what society says we should do. How can I, as a leader of my household, a big bad NFL player, be open about my most intimate secrets and feelings? *Yikes!* How can I express my fears and self-proclaimed failures while maintaining my bravado and machismo?

We live in a world where we are expected to always look as if we have it all together, and everything is perfect. I'm supposed to have the answers. I'm supposed to be the protector and provider who knows what the next steps are. It's very challenging to go against the grain and openly discuss our flaws. *Men, you feel me?*

KING OF COMEDY

My wife and I have had many discussions about my lack of openness in certain areas involving my feelings toward her and our children. One instance that comes to mind was when I couldn't stop being Mr. King of Comedy. I literally had a joke for everyone and every situation regardless of how it made someone feel. I figured making jokes was good for everyone because who doesn't like to laugh, right?

The problem was when you continue to joke on the same people continuously, they accumulate a lot of negative wounds. And for me, my wife and children were always on the receiving end of my jokes. It was so bad my wife became fed up with my constant joking on her, and she communicated with me about how I hardly spoke nicely to her and how everything I said to her involved sarcasm or she was always at the end of my jokes. She ultimately didn't feel good about it, and when I think about it from her perspective, who the heck would want to always be the punchline of jokes by their significant other? All the jokes that I thought were funny and lightening the mood were actually having a negative effect on her because I wasn't doing what a husband should be doing, which is uplifting and empowering his wife!

Now I'm not saying providing comic relief isn't sometimes a good thing. It's definitely necessary for life, but too much of anything can create negative results, and that's what was happening. The Bible talks about how you have the power of life and death in the tongue, and I wasn't speaking life into my wife. Unfortunately, I was speaking death to her dreams, confidence, and overall spirit all because I thought I was a comedian. It took her expressing her displeasure with me in this area for me to start to realize what I was doing.

I initially was offended because I thought how could she take the jokes to heart, especially when she knew how I felt about her, but the problem was she didn't hear my true feelings. She was hearing my jokes, which didn't include positivity and highlighting her successes. My jokes always included her shortcomings and flaws. After a while, that gets old. It wasn't easy for me to hear this, nor was it easy for me to adjust to this, but it was absolutely mandatory. I had to make a conscious decision to speak life into my wife and my children.

I made the mental rule that for every one negative joke, I would highlight three things that I loved about my wife or children afterward so they could still hear something positive and know that I truly love them. It's funny when I think about this rule because it seems pretty simple, but it was very difficult for me at the beginning because I love to joke. When I get going, I think I'm Eddie Murphy or Bernie Mac. The problem is when you continue to use all your joking skills on one person, it turns into a form of bullying, and it leads to that person feeling insecure, which is unacceptable, especially in a marriage. Now, this is still something I have to continue working on, but the dynamic of my family is drastically better now than before I started using the 1:3 rule.

Another thing I struggled with was discussing the goals that I had set for myself when I fell short of them. It was difficult to become self-aware and acknowledge that I was fundamentally flawed in this area due to a lifetime of suppressing my feelings and intimate secrets.

A little bit of pride and insecurity had kept a veil over my eyes regarding my lack of openness. And when that veil came down, my pride had to come down with it. I knew that if I didn't address the root issues behind my lack of authenticity, my relationships would suffer, and the health of my family would deteriorate over time.

I had to admit that I could not hold it all together. I had to be honest about my fears and emotions with those who were closest to me. I had to stop assuming that everything rested on my shoulders. We have spouses for a reason. We carry the burden together. We have a circle of trusted friends for a reason. We encourage one another on the path of life. We pick each other up when we fall. And we share our thoughts and fears so we don't feel quite so alone.

After acknowledging that I had an openness problem, I had to create a plan to help me commit to being more open and find ways to hold myself accountable. This whole process was very daunting at first, but I remembered one of my favorite quotes that always seems to apply to my life when I'm facing a tough task.

It's from the ancient Chinese philosopher Lao-tzu. "The journey of a thousand miles begins with a single step." When I thought about that quote, it instantly inspired me to take the first step to be more open with my family. I decided I had to take the jump!

TAKING OFF THE MASK

I started small with being honest when my wife would ask me if I was tired or not. Up to that point 99 percent of the time I would answer her with "Nope. I feel great." That would be my answer even if I were extremely tired because I couldn't appear weak in any regard. I believed the lie that if I appeared weak, then I was not fulfilling my duty as a husband and father.

Step number one for me was honesty when she asked me that question. I told her the truth about being tired even though I felt so uncomfortable saying it because I was determined to be more vulnerable. I was humbling myself and purposely exposing a flaw in Mr. Perfection even though it was going against everything I had been mentally conditioned to do! It may seem like a small task to some, but this initial step of humility started me on the journey to openness and authenticity with my wife.

Imagine my surprise when it carried over to me being more open with my children. What dad doesn't want to be a superhero to their kids? I certainly did. I thought that if I could fulfill the role of Mr. Perfection, I was protecting them. As I began to be more honest about my flaws with them, I thought they would be disappointed because my Mr. Perfect persona costume would start to fade. But instead, as I became more open, they began to truly see who their father was, and they began to have a deeper understanding of me. When they can see who I am, they have a better understanding of who they are. My openness has brought them strength. It has brought them a more secure identity. They didn't need Mr. Perfection to protect them. They needed an authentic dad, flaws and all.

The funny thing is when we have to step out of our comfort zone and become vulnerable, we truly psych ourselves out, and the fear of the action is actually way worse than the action itself!

By deciding to be more open with my family, I opened the door for us to become closer. My wife and children started being more open with me. All of this created a new layer of understanding we had with each other.

Now, by no stretch of the imagination, are we a perfect family. We're not completely open about absolutely everything. We're not that perfect TV sitcom family in the least! We still have our struggles and disagreements, and sometimes our overall dynamic is just plain off. But the one thing I can say, due to our focused approach on being more open with one another, we can communicate our issues a lot better and with a lot more understanding. This ultimately leads us to resolve our differences swiftly before they grow into something larger than they should be.

THE OTHER SIDE OF THE WALL

I cannot stress to you enough how important openness is to the success of a marriage, relationship, and/or family. When those emotional walls are present, not only does it prevent people from getting in, but it doesn't allow people to see the real you. Emotional walls keep you from expressing yourself truly and freely, which is key to you being your best self!

An emotional wall is a self-defense mechanism. We feel we need to guard our feelings, but sometimes the things we think are helping us are actually hurting us. Remaining guarded because we believe it's the safe thing to do is actually causing us to be more isolated and wounding us further.

We use walls to prevent ourselves from experiencing pain and from being let down. We use walls to keep from being disappointed or deceived. But these walls are cutting off our oxygen. They are preventing true comfort. Walls that we thought would keep us safe are cutting us off from the relationships we need to heal. All of this takes me back to my initial question, Are you really LIVING?

Being alive and actually living are two different things. Living life in the "safe" category because you never take chances is not truly living. Trying to protect yourself from failure or heartache will cause you to live a false life inside an isolated prison.

Failure is part of living. As hard as it is to admit, heartache is part of living. Bringing your walls down will allow the possibility of failure and heartache. But it will also open up the possibility of learning to fly!

I want to tell you from the other side of the wall. It's okay to fail. It really is. It's how we learn and grow. There's freedom in failing. Because you know what? Every person on earth has failed at something. Some of us have failed spectacularly. *Yours truly!* But hey, we get up, we learn from it. We ask for forgiveness, and we move on. This process is much better than trying to keep our walls intact and Mr. Perfection on the throne of his false perfect life.

I've learned that on the other side of the wall that it's okay to experience heartache. It's okay to jump and fall flat on my face. There are reasons for all of these things—they bring us to a true understanding of real life and how to navigate. There is a strength that is gained when we face failure and heartache. We process the pain. We process the failure. And in the process, we become more.

When we experience and process real life, we become who we were meant to be. If we hide behind our emotional walls, we will never grow, never really be known, and never experience true life.

As we bring down our walls and process our pain, we gain wisdom and understanding. We gain maturity through the experience. We also become more fearless, knowing we can handle the pain, knowing we can process the failure, knowing that our worth doesn't lie in our wins and our losses. Our worth lies in the unconditional love we give and receive. Our worth comes from our Creator.

On the other side of the wall, you will experience inspiration, hope, and purpose. Not only will you be alive, but you will be LIVING!

Not being authentic with the people you love and care about will not only hinder you, it will also hinder them from being able to experience life with you on a deeper level. The world deserves to have you and what you offer to it. The world needs whatever it is you've been put here to accomplish. Because we all have a purpose.

Openness will be a difficult step. It was for me. But I can tell you, no matter how difficult this step is and no matter how many times you will want to throw in the towel, it will be worth it. I know that fear will try to keep you from taking that first step. And fear will lie to you and tell you that being open about your feelings will cause more headaches and arguments than if you just remained guarded and put on your "everything is perfect" mask.

Here's what I can tell you: Even though it's tough, if you just continue to step out of your comfort zone and be open and honest, if you deliver your message in the correct manner with patience, humility, and love, you will experience a connection unlike any other. And this openness will ultimately bring you strength because you are becoming who you were created to be.

Love comes when manipulation stops; when you think more about the other person than about his or her reactions to you. When you dare to reveal yourself fully. When you dare to be vulnerable.

—Dr. Joyce Brothers

CHAPTER

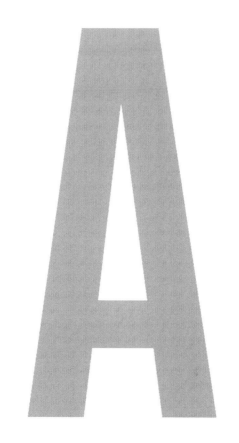

Actively

INSPIRE OTHERS

If you're not making someone else's life better, then you're wasting your time. Your life will become better by making other lives better.

—Will Smith

INSPIRATION PRODUCES INSPIRATION

What do Leonardo DaVinci, Shakespeare, Jean-Michel Basquiat, Jay-Z, Beyoncé, Michael Jordan, and Barack Obama have in common? They were all inspired to become great and in turn, inspired others!

All of these people had someone strike a match in them that lit their creativity and set their dreams on fire. That creativity shone like a light in the darkness, and as their dreams came true, they gave hope to many. The world changed because of them. But first, someone had to spark the idea within them that they could do something great with the life and talents they had been given.

People who change the world have one thing in common: Someone challenged their mental, emotional, and personal creativity to go after their dreams. They were inspired.

When the artist or leader becomes inspired to become all they can be, they create things that have never been created before. Others who watch their creativity bloom into fulfilled dreams are inspired to grow to their fullest potential. It's like a fire that catches from one person to the next.

Somewhere our inner child comes alive, and we BELIEVE we were meant for more. We BELIEVE there is something inside of us that was meant to shine in the world, and if we only pursue it and develop that creativity, we, too, can change the world and inspire others to change it.

Inspiration is what makes a kid growing up in the Tidewater Area of Virginia have hope that he can do great things in the world.

Anything great that has ever happened or been created has come from inspiration!

MY PERSONAL HEROES

I was very fortunate to have both of my parents in my life growing up. A lot of my friends did not. But the inner city was rough.

I remember one of the first houses I lived in growing up was formerly a crack house. My parents were able to get the house at a very low price, and it had a ton of potential to be a nice house. The only problem was it had most recently been used as a drug house, and that meant it needed a ton of work before it was suitable for a family to live in. I remember cleaning up human feces off the floor. And we saw so many rats that we began naming them. We eventually transformed the house into a nice home, but all inner-city homes have issues, and we were just another home on that long list.

During that whole process, I remember my father inspiring me the most as a former Marine. He always had the mentality that no matter how rough it is, it's always going to turn out positive. Regardless of what the situation we may be in, we're always going to come out on top.

We faced quite a bit of adversity growing up in the inner-city community. We couldn't go to the next street over because drug dealers lived there. People were getting killed. I couldn't go visit my cousins down the street because there were too many dangerous things happening on that street.

But my dad always faced adversity with a smile. I'm sure there were plenty of times that he felt pressured by a negative situation, but that never kept him from smiling. None of the hard times kept him from pressing toward the mark.

I remember one day, a drug head was running from the police. He jumped on our porch and tried to get into our house. My father was like, "Heck no! You're not coming in here!" He kicked the drug head off the porch. Not even 30 seconds later, a police officer ran onto our porch, but he thought that the guy was still in the house because he couldn't find him. My father got into an argument with the officer.

The officer was cursing my dad out. I had never seen my dad talked to like that because he's a Marine. People in our neighborhood did not address him in that manner. But I watched how he addressed the officer respectfully but also very sternly to let him know that my dad was not going to be talked to like that. He could have been fearful; he could have acted less humanely with a physical altercation, but my dad had been trained to understand how to first connect with a person, and then use his words to set boundaries for the situation. He was respectful, but he was obviously not going to let himself be run over by the police officer.

I initially thought, *Man, I hate all police officers. My dad did nothing wrong, and yet he was accused and verbally accosted.* But all these years later, what actually took root in my heart was my dad's mind-set—to be calm and collected, and yet not fold in tense situations.

Another personal inspiration of mine is Dr. Martin Luther King Jr. I saw that same kind of strength in him that I saw in my father. Even though he faced so much adversity, he was able to stay true to his doctrine. He stayed true to his core. It's difficult to learn to not retaliate. It's difficult to not react in haste to injustice. But honestly, negative retaliation is the easy way out. Dr. Martin Luther King Jr. kept to his doctrine of nonviolence even when he was persecuted, physically assaulted, and knocked around simply because he was try-ing to be a voice for the voiceless. It's just so inspiring. He impacted the nation and ultimately changed the trajectory for the culture of African Americans.

MY OWN DOCTRINE

As I began my career in football, I developed my own doctrine. In the end, no matter what praise I got for being a football player, it was more important to me to be a great man. Even though I wanted to be in the NFL since I was four years old, it was more important for me to leave a lasting impact on others. I wanted to be a legend in life, not just a football hero on the field.

I remember that quote from the movie *The Sandlot.* "Heroes get remembered, but legends never die."

I want the things I do here on earth to continue growing and manifesting for future generations. I want to be a wave maker when it comes to actively inspiring others. That's what Dr. Martin Luther King Jr. did for me. His wave lives in me. I want to do that for others. He is my example, and I strive to repeat his success.

Another one of my inspirations might seem a little strange to some, but when I was growing up, there was a guy who made it out of my hometown and became a big star athlete. Allen Iverson came from my neck of the woods, and as a kid looking up to him, he was a beast to me. He had to overcome the stereotypes and adversity of the inner city to become a star player in the NBA.

As I looked at him, I saw that he had braids. I had braids. He had tattoos. I had tattoos. He was just like me. He came from the same place that I did, and he made it! I began to think, *If he can become a professional athlete, why can't I become a professional athlete? If he can overcome this adversity, why can't I?*

I remember watching him play in the NBA finals. I can't tell you the feeling of watching someone from my hometown playing at the height of his sport on national television! It inspired me to believe in myself. It inspired me to believe that anything was possible. Nothing was standing in the way of me being able to reach that same level as far as being a professional athlete.

I vividly remember two other people that I drew inspiration: Rosa Parks and my mother. The things that stood out to me the most about them were the fact that they didn't have a prominent standing in society, nor were they star athletes or physically imposing for that matter. The thing I admired most about these women was that they didn't let the status quo affect their ability to take action and make a difference.

When Rosa Parks decided not to give up her seat and go to the back of the bus, she didn't do so because she was a big name in the community and everyone would succumb to her demand. She did so because she was tired of how everything had been. She was tired of how African-Americans were being treated. She was ultimately tired of people not standing up for what they believed in. So she decided to take action. That took a ton of courage. I would think about the courage of Rosa Parks when I would face challenges. I would think about her courage when I left the Tidewater Area of Virginia, which was predominantly African-American and ventured to James Madison University, which was drastically different. I understood what I was venturing to do was bigger than me. It would be the biggest step outside my comfort zone up to that point in my life.

What I was going to do would open doors for the next generation and ultimately be a beacon of hope to the hopeless. A sign to the youth in my city that it is possible to be successful. A message that if you want to change something, you have to find the courage to take action just like Rosa Parks did.

When I think about my mother becoming the first woman pastor at a very prominent Baptist church in the Tidewater Area, I think about the scrutiny she faced and all the negatives associated with being the first to do something that hadn't been done in a hundred years! I think about how she didn't let the negativity deter her away from her goal of spreading the gospel and impacting lives. I think about how she could've easily thrown in the towel when she faced the politics associated with the position and the lack of support she received. Instead, she found the courage to stand up to the status quo and the stigma against woman pastors. She found the courage to say I will not let this storm keep me from receiving my blessing.

My mother ultimately decided that she, just like Rosa Parks, would simply make a decision to do what others said couldn't be done. The courage found in these two women is something I admire and to this day still draw inspiration from.

None of the people who inspired me were perfect. I am not wearing rose-colored glasses concerning their flaws. But it's to my advantage to learn from their mistakes as well. I not only learn from the positives but also the negatives. Maybe they were powerful at their calling but missed it when it came to being husbands and fathers. Maybe a few of them could have avoided some pain by taking different steps. Or they could have dealt with certain controversies with less emotion and evoked a better outcome. Even though I stand on the shoulders of flawed men, they are the people who sparked the fire within me. They are my inspiration. And I am forever grateful.

MY LITTLE BROTHER BRIAN

As I grew older, I carried this passion for actively inspiring others. I wanted to be intentional. I wanted to create the same waves of inspiration in others that my heroes started in me.

In college, I began to look for ways to get more involved. I heard about an organization called Big Brothers Big Sisters, which is a mentoring organization for young adolescents who are at risk. As a Big Brother, you become a mentor to a young child by connecting with them on a weekly basis. A lot of these kids come from broken homes. This program really spoke to my heart. It was right up my alley with my desire to help disadvantaged youth.

So, when I signed up to be a Big Brother, I was going into my junior year of college. I told them at the time I could speak Spanish. Let's just say I *thought* I could speak Spanish. *I might have been a little overconfident!*

They paired me with this little brother named Brian. He was six years old, and he had no father in his life. The rest of his family was strictly Spanish speaking. It was a very limiting situation in terms of Brian being set up to be successful. All the odds were stacked against him. None of his family members were high school graduates. No one spoke English. And there was no dad in his life. I walked in the first day, met him, and did my best to explain to his mom that I was Arthur from JMU. *I'm sure my broken Spanish wasn't helping instill any confidence in me.*

If you can picture this: I was an African American college kid with braids trying to communicate in broken Spanish that I was with Big Brothers Big Sisters and wanted to take her six-year-old son and mentor him. *I can only imagine what she must've thought.*

Let's just say that I had to grow immediately in my knowledge of Spanish and how to use it properly. I felt so uncomfortable speaking Spanish to a person who only speaks Spanish. I desperately wanted to communicate enough to let her know that everything would be alright, and I was trustworthy. But it all worked out, and I started hanging out with Brian.

So, I would pick up her son and spend some time with him. It was just crazy because there were times when my college roommates were like, "Yo, who is this? There's a Mexican kid sitting on the counter." I would explain that he was my little brother.

Brian began to see that somebody cared enough about him to take time out of their day just for him. Sometimes I would call him, just to make sure he was doing his homework. There were times I would help him with his homework.

As a college athlete going into my junior season, it would have been easy to live the "big man on campus" lifestyle, but I couldn't do that. It's not what made me a better person. It's not what made me happy. I decided to invest even more time with Brian. Our relationship grew, and he went from a kid who was getting bad grades and headed down an unsuccessful path to a kid who slowly made some positive changes because he was being pointed in a positive direction. He began to see that he could make a difference in his life, and he could become the first person in his family to graduate.

There came a time when we lost contact because his family didn't have any cell phones or a house phone, and they would have to move and go live with a relative. I would have to drive around and find him. We went through a time when we weren't connected, and I had to contact Big Brothers Big Sisters to find him.

I was able to connect with him just a few years ago. He was able to express how much those times with me meant to him. He had a picture of us, and he said it was such a great reminder of how someone really believed in him.

After we reconnected, I found out he had had a bout with cancer, And because of the depression that came along with it, he had some suicidal thoughts. He said, "I would think back to some of the positive things you told me, and I decided that I WAS somebody. I was important. Ultimately it helped me go through this process."

Walking down memory lane with him was so incredible. It was the why behind what I did. It's about impacting lives. He knew I was real, and my motives were pure. I can't tell you what an awesome feeling I had knowing that the time I invested was worth every moment.

Success is less about fame or fortune and more about the lives that you have an impact on. Just a few weeks ago, I was able to go to his high school graduation on his birthday. He was the first person who graduated from high school in his family.

He said, "You started this relationship when I was six. Not only did you take time with me back then, but you took time away from your family to come to Harrisonburg, Virginia, to my high school graduation. That means everything to me."

It was very inspirational for me because he was like, *Wow, like you're really doing what you set out to do, and you're really a person of your word.*

I'm always a believer that if I'm doing something, I really want to have that positive impact. I love changing the trajectory of people's lives for the better. And this was one of those full-circle moments.

I am passionate about actively inspiring others. You'll never really know what a difference just pouring a little of your time into someone will make.

SPARKING GREATNESS

Since inspiration is the foundation for all things great, I want to talk about actively seeking ways to inspire your family and others. What will spark them to reach their highest potential? What will click within their soul and launch the ideas that are locked up within them? How can their minds be widened to the possibilities that are available to them?

There was an interesting side effect that happened as I gave back to the community, several of my teammates throughout my career began to come along with me.

I did not follow the typical path of being an NFL player. I knew that athletes have a much bigger purpose than football. My teammates would take notice that I had chosen to walk a little differently. It was important for me to inspire my teammates—that we needed to be more than just great football players. We needed to be good husbands and dads. We needed to be better men. Football has a shelf life. But the rest of what we do for our family and community is what has a long-lasting real-life impact.

I've had teammates come back to me and say, "I decided to go back and get my master's degree because of you. I saw you doing it while you played and told myself I had no excuse not to go for it." I never even mentioned to others that they should go back to school. They were simply inspired because they saw me conquer the mountain.

I can't stress to you enough the importance that inspiration will have not only on your family but on our communities, our nation, and then the world! We never know the impact our inspiration will have on someone and the potential great things they will accomplish.

FULL-CIRCLE MOMENTS

The other side to inspiring others is the feeling of gratitude and satisfaction you experience when you realize that your inspiration helped an individual achieve success. I can speak from experience when I say it's euphoric when someone tells you about something they accomplished all because they were inspired by you to do it.

Throughout my nine-year NFL career, I was blessed with the opportunity to see firsthand the pure joy of inspiration. I think back to my rookie season in the NFL when I held a free football skills camp at my high school in Portsmouth, Virginia. It was important for me to make sure it was completely free because I knew how many of the youth in that area couldn't participate in certain events due to a lack of financial resources.

At my first day of camp, I always made sure the theme was clear to everyone in attendance. If you set your mind to achieve greatness in anything and you commit 100 percent of your efforts to it, you will attain it. I made it a point to look every participant in the eye and tell them that message and let them know that I was living proof. It's one thing to talk about it, but I wanted to make sure they could see a perfect example of what I was preaching.

At the time, I had no clue what would come of the individuals who heard that message at my camp. But what I did know was that I was planting a seed of hope that their current circumstances didn't have to dictate their future. I knew that when they left the camp, they would be able to say, "If Arthur Moats can do it, I can do it. Because he came from the same place, I came from." Circumstances are no excuse not to try.

Fast-forward eight years to 2018, I had just completed my eighth season in the NFL. I had been asked to be the keynote speaker at the CAA Football Conference Media Day. As I was at the media day meeting with the collegiate athletes, press, and various coaches, I ran across a face that didn't look familiar to me. However, this young man told me that he knew me from our hometown in the "757" or the Tidewater Area of Virginia. I was slightly puzzled, but I asked the young man to tell me how he knew me, and this is where I was blown away.

Now mind you, I'm at the CAA media day where the top collegiate athletes from the conference are in attendance to receive various preseason awards and accolades. This is a pretty big deal. He then told me he attended my football camps that I held at my high school when he was younger and that he was inspired to seriously pursue a career in football and had received a scholarship to the University of Towson. He was going into his senior season where he had been an All-CAA selection! As he's telling me all of this, I'm thinking, *This is incredible! Who would've thought my words would have had this level of impact on a person? And how fortunate for me to see this come to fruition!* It was an experience that brought me a mixture of joy, pride, genuine happiness, and fulfillment. It was like that feeling you get after a hard day of work, but you're so proud of what you were able to accomplish, so you just sit and smile without saying a word. It was a full-circle moment for me.

To this day, that is one of my proudest moments because it encompasses everything I want my life to be about: to be an inspiration for people to achieve greatness! Every day I wake up, I want to be an inspiration to every person who interacts with me directly and indirectly. I feel if I inspire enough people to do great things, and, in turn, they inspire other people to do great things, in the end the world will be a better place and filled with people living up to their full potential.

Now when I speak of greatness and achieving it, I understand that every person's greatness is specifically tailored to that individual. One person's greatness and potential will never be the same as someone else's, so it's important to never compare your value to someone else because we are all uniquely, fearfully, and wonderfully made!

Let's not settle for the world being as it is and feel powerless against the status quo. Let's be the change we want to see in the world and inspire as many people as possible to achieve their greatness and have a positive impact on their lives. Be intentional about inspiring others. Be the spark that lights someone else's flame, and watch the world catch on fire!

Those who are happiest are those who do the most for others.
—Booker T. Washington

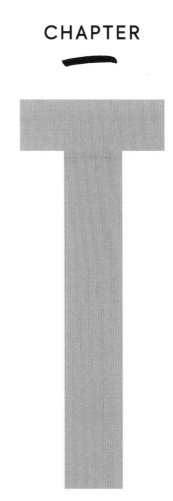

FEAR INTO FOCUS

Never let the fear of striking out get in your way.

—Babe Ruth

EARLY CHOICES

I grew up in the inner-city area in two very rough neighborhoods: Campostella and Park Place in Norfolk, Virginia. They are historically known for a lot of criminal activity and drug infestation. From time to time, we experienced a bit of police brutality and injustice, which I witnessed firsthand.

My parents sacrificed nice paying jobs in sales to work in ministry there. They knew their calling was in ministry, and even though it meant walking away from financial security, they were committed to walking in their purpose. When I look back at the circumstances, it truly amazes me that they were able to keep a roof over our heads and food on our plates. My parents did whatever it took to be sure that my siblings and I knew that we had value, despite our rough circumstances. I experienced coming home to the candles lit at four in the afternoon because our lights were shut off, and I remember seeing an eviction notice. But even though we had a rough situation, some people had it much worse than we did. There is one thing I'll never forget through all the struggles of growing up. My parents instilled in my siblings and me this simple thought, "You are somebody because God doesn't create junk." That was our family mantra through every financial hardship we experienced. The impact of that statement had a profound effect on me. Lack of finances does not imply a lack of worth.

As a young man, I knew I had worth, but all the outward circumstances—the crime, the drugs, the injustice, along with my parents' financial situation—created a fight-or-flight mentality in my mind. It created a deep desire in me to get out.

I made a vow to myself that I was NOT going to live in this kind of insecurity. I thought, *I'm going to get an education and be successful. I'm not going to go through these things when I'm older.* I don't want to face eviction or the possibility of my car being repossessed. I hated it when one bag of chips had to last the whole week. I know my parents did the best they could because of their calling to ministry, but it created a fighter in me. I wanted a better life.

I saw friends of mine become rich by dealing drugs. They got to wear nice clothes and have nice cars. I saw that drugs could be a path out of poverty. But I also saw them go to jail and even get killed. My cousin was a drug dealer and told me early on, "This is not what you wanna do, man." He made me promise him that I would never touch a drug to either use or sell, and that was a promise I kept. He saw I had a focus to change my life, and he was warning me that this was not the path I wanted to take. I understood what he meant when six months later he was killed.

This wake-up call helped me to realize that I was focusing so much on the things I didn't want my life to be that I wasn't actually focusing on what I needed to become. If we always fear what the future brings, then we're not focused on making the future all that it can be. Concentrating on your goals and hustling to reach them is a much better response than worrying about what the future holds.

I didn't want to live in poverty anymore. I didn't want to end up dead at twenty-two like my cousin. So, I had to ask myself some questions: Was I ready to pay the price and climb this mountain? Was I going to be stuck in fear on this level my whole life? Or was I going to concentrate on my grades and my athletic talent and begin to climb the mountain in front of me?

I decided to focus on what I wanted to accomplish. I wanted to be a great husband. I want to be a highly successful football player. I wanted to create generational wealth, not only monetarily but also inner strength and security for my children and their children.

It was important for me to make sure that my family didn't have to walk so closely to the crime and the drugs. At the same time, from my standpoint of security, I wanted to be able to reach back into those communities and help where I could.

If I could focus on creating a firm foundation for myself, I would be able to go back and help those who were hurting and discouraged. I would be able to be a positive example of making a better life. The inner city has a ton of examples of people trying to do it the wrong way. But I thought, *What if I could do it the right way and come back and impact some kids through the inner-city youth programs? What if I could turn this fear I have into a focus that inspires others to be better dads and better men?* I had a goal to escape the insecurity of the inner city, but I also had a goal to go back and be a beacon of hope for those who needed it.

It was a lot of pressure. Being "the good guy" is a lot of pressure, but I look to those who have gone before me, and they did it the right way. People like Martin Luther King Jr. put it all on the line to give the people a light in the darkness. He turned fear into focus. If I have to put myself out there and be vulnerable to give another person some inspiration and hope, I'm okay with that. The pressure is worth it. The payoff comes when you change someone's life.

RISKY MOVES

We've all experienced fear at one time or another. I'm not referring to that fear you get while watching a super spooky scary movie when the killer is hiding in the closet and jumps out, making you and every person in the room jump out of their skin. I'm referring to the fear that keeps you from reaching your greatest potential in life.

The fear that makes you second-guess yourself or find ways to justify not pursuing something you're truly passionate about because "it doesn't make sense." The fear that makes you stay at one job for years knowing you're not happy because "it's safe and pays well." The fear that makes you stay in a relationship with someone far too long because "at least I know what I'm getting from them." The fear that paralyzes you from ever taking a chance on yourself and jumping out of your safe zone—that's the fear I'm talking about.

The fear that keeps us from taking risks is very real, and by no stretch of the imagination is it easy to overcome. There were plenty of times I was paralyzed by it. Even though people looking at me on the surface saw success, I knew I was nowhere near my full potential.

I have two competing mind-sets. I am a master planner where I love for each and every step to be planned out, so I know exactly what is going to happen next. And then I have this other crazy, reckless, spontaneous mind-set that says, "Just take the leap, you'll learn to fly!"

But these two mind-sets don't mesh well together. They have proved to be extremely difficult to master. It's a little bit like swinging on a pendulum. At one moment, I'm ready to leap and risk everything on a whim. But in the next moment, I feel as if I can't take a step because I haven't figured out every nuance and future challenge that will present itself.

On top of that, when you factor in having a family with children, it makes the risky steps even harder to accomplish. When you have other people depending on you, if you fail, they fail with you.

It would seem as a professional football player that one of the biggest pressures I had to face was playing in a prime-time game against Tom Brady. The stakes were extremely high. The pressure was huge to prevent him from putting together a miraculous comeback drive in front of millions of fans.

But honestly, that doesn't even move the needle when compared to being a newlywed with a six-year-old daughter and three-month-old, while just finishing up your contract with the Buffalo Bills. My inner master planner did not like the feeling of sitting on the free agency market that has gone cold because inside linebacker isn't a priority. It also doesn't help calm the nerves of my master planner when I get a phone call from Mike Tomlin saying, "Come to Pittsburgh on a one-year vet minimum 'prove it' deal. But I can't give you any guarantees, and I already have my starters in place, oh yeah, and you're going to have to switch positions and beat out some guys."

Now that's pressure! You want to talk about the fear of failing turning into paralysis, that's it right there! My first thought was, *How the heck am I going to tell my wife about this job opportunity that has no assurances it will last more than a year and expect her to be happy about it?* Having a newborn is stressful enough, but then when you factor in the uncertainty of employment along with having to make a big move with your family to another state, to another job that includes zero guarantees, this can become your worst fear.

There was so much risk involved with these decisions. To fail in this situation would change the trajectory of my family. Failure could have had a lasting negative effect on my relationship with my wife and the future of my children as well.

These were the negative thoughts running through my mind after the phone call with Coach Tomlin. As much as I would like to say that I played it cool, I was honestly scared. The uncertainty of my job security was causing me to shrink back in fear. My internal dialogue centered around weighing the risks of failure. I soon realized that if I let the negative self-talk win, I was actually letting failure win instead of standing up to conquer it.

Fear felt like it was too big to overcome, but I decided it was not going to get the best of me. I was going to meet this giant head on and push back against the darkness in my mind.

The first thing I did was prioritize and put things into perspective. What would bring me the most happiness? Would I be happy choosing to play it safe? I could try and find employment in the Buffalo job market since I had spent the previous four years there, or would it make me happy to take a chance on life and do something that most would deem crazy?

I did have to look at all sides of the situation. What would I truly be risking? If I found something slow, steady, and secure, where no one would have their routines altered drastically, was that my definition of success and happiness? Or did I need to take the leap by picking up the family and moving to a different state while hoping and praying that this risk would pay off? Was it the right decision to take a massive chance on myself and my skills and accomplish something that would bring financial freedom to my family and children? After I had clearly laid out the situation in my mind, I decided to look at the mountain called fear and tell it to move.

I decided it was worth taking a chance on myself. I didn't feel like I was done playing football; I had more to give and the game had more to give to me. And even though this seemed like an unsafe route for my family, I needed to take a leap and trust that my story was going to play out just like it should.

Honestly, it could've backfired on me, and for a while, I thought it did. But I continued to believe in myself and refused to allow my fear of failure to keep me from trying. I wish I could say that me telling the mountain of fear to move was a one and done conversation. But fear doesn't usually listen the first time. I had to tell that mountain to move several more times before it decided I was serious!

Instead of focusing on the possibility of failure, I took my fear and turned it into focus at my workplace. I became so focused on improving as a player and a person that the only option, in the end, was for me to become my best self. When I look back on that decision and the growth I experienced during that time, I smile. It was all turned for my good! I was able to overcome a fear that a lot of people never overcome. I was able to do something special not only for myself but for my family as well. I was able to have a larger impact on more communities and lives because of this decision. My platform and reach became larger than I could've ever imagined.

FACING GOLIATH

You never know when your opportunity is going to come, but when it does come, you have to make sure that you've put the necessary work in and the necessary time in to ultimately make it successful. You have to not waste time in any season of life to be prepared for the sudden opportunities that present themselves. Often, people will become discouraged about a negative situation in their lives. They'll slow down in the valleys and feel sorry for themselves when they should be using that time to prepare for the next unseen opportunity.

When I came to Pittsburgh from Buffalo, I faced a valley that was filled with possible, fearful outcomes. Professionally, I had played 80 percent of my defensive snaps as an inside linebacker for multiple years. And then to have to leave and go to a different team, switching divisions, switching positions, put my mind in a whirlwind.

In my personal life, my wife recently had our second baby, and now we were moving to a completely different part of the country. All of this, coupled with the fact that my job was very unstable. I only got five snaps in my first two games as a Steeler. I feared that if this job didn't work out for me, my family was going to find itself on unstable ground financially.

My internal dialogue at that point was questioning all the decisions I had made: *Maybe I should have taken the deal with Cleveland instead. Maybe I should have followed my defensive coordinator. I'm going to be out of the league if I don't make this work. God, please let this work out!*

The valley has a way of revealing your level of maturity. It's in the valley that you learn who you are. All the ugly stuff comes to the top, and you can deal with it, or you can sweep it under the rug. If you sweep it under the rug, you won't be ready for the opportunities that come your way. If you don't deal with the ugly stuff, it simply means it's going to come up again. You might as well deal with it the first time.

I remember having a pregame meal with my family. We were going into my third game as a Steeler. My mom and her husband at the time were with us for that *Sunday Night Football* game in Carolina. They were pointing out some really good truths to me about how I'd been handling the valley. They pointed out that I had chosen to stay focused. They pointed to the fact that I kept studying my playbook. I watched tons of film. I did tons of workouts. I was keeping my body hydrated. I was keeping myself ready for the opportunity even in this discouraging part of the season.

I didn't know when it was going to happen, but when my opportunity came, I wanted to capitalize on it. I wanted to make sure that I could make the most of it. I thought, *I would regret it forever if an opportunity came, but I missed it because I was having a pity party.* It would kill me to know that I gave up in the valley because things weren't working out the way I thought they should. I was determined to be ready for the opportunities that presented themselves.

Fast-forward to the actual game against the Carolina Panthers. Within the first few quarters, Jarvis Jones broke his wrist. So then, my number was called.

The opportunity I've been preparing for was here. It was time to get up and do what I knew how to do. It was time to produce for my team. It was time to join the fight on the field. I knew my plays. I knew my opponent. My body was ready, and so was my mind. I stepped on the field and got a big sack on their quarterback, Cam Newton. It was a surreal moment. I had a very productive game, and ultimately, we came out with a win. My success that game changed the trajectory of the rest of my time in Pittsburgh. It ultimately opened the door for a three-year contract extension. I was ready because I didn't let the valley consume me.

I've always called it my David and Goliath moment. Think about David when he was preparing in the field, as a shepherd boy, tending to his sheep. He was doing the stuff that no one wanted to give him respect for. No one talked about him. There was no fanfare. He didn't know why he was doing it, but he knew he had to do it.

He rescued the sheep from a bear. He rescued the sheep from a lion. He kept having to rescue the sheep from everything! He didn't know that he was practicing for an opportunity that was soon to come his way. Goliath was waiting to be taken down, and God was preparing an unassuming warrior to do just that.

David had to face Goliath to open the door to his destiny. He overcame. He got the credit for his preparation. He grew into the man God created him to be. He didn't let the disrespect of his brothers and family get in his way. He didn't let what other people thought of him create a prison of shame around him. He just kept practicing for his opportunity. And God brought it about at the right time.

This Goliath moment came for me during the Carolina game. I was ready. But during the preparation, I had to focus on not letting all of my negative thinking take root in me. I didn't focus on the pay cut I had to take. I didn't focus on the fact that I saw very little playing time those first two games. I just stayed ready. And the perfect opportunity came during a *Sunday Night Football* game. My number was called. I helped my team succeed, and I was able to make my mark again. It felt like I was visible to people again. This paid off financially down the road when I signed my three-year contract extension. It was the most money that I'd ever seen in my life! My family was now financially set.

I focused on preparing for my opportunity. It's the perfect example of turning my fear into focus. In the end, just like David, it paid off!

MOUNTAIN CLIMBING

It's truly an amazing feeling to overcome my fear. I am humbled at what I was able to accomplish after that mountain moved, and I am so thankful I got to experience what was on the other side. The mountain is now a molehill. But it took me standing up to fear and choosing to focus on what I knew I was called to do.

Climbing mountains in your life can be very challenging because in the midst of climbing you typically can't see the top. You usually don't see how close you are to reaching the peak. All you know is that you're tired, frustrated, and starting to question whether you will ever get there. This stage is extremely hard for people like me who are very goal oriented. We focus all our efforts on getting to the top. When things don't happen according to our timetable, we begin to become frustrated and fed up. We ask ourselves questions like, What would make you think you're good enough to accomplish this? What makes you different from every other person who has failed? Why don't you just quit and make more realistic goals? These are all questions I've asked myself numerous times while climbing my various mountains, and honestly the only thing that helped me keep going was me pausing for a second and looking at where I was.

One mistake I had to learn to overcome was to stop looking so far ahead. I needed to focus on the situation around me, and what needed to be done on the level I was at. Looking up to where I was going at the moment seemed too far and was too discouraging. But it helped to acknowledge where I was on the mountain in comparison to where I had started.

Gaining perspective while mountain climbing gave me the ability to see that even though I wasn't where I desired to be at the moment, I was a lot further along than when I started. I was able to see that if I just kept taking one step at a time, I could accomplish the unthinkable. I could do what people said couldn't be done. I could be that 1 percent that makes it to the NFL, without being a nationally ranked high school recruit or playing at a major Division 1 college university.

One Bible verse I fell in love with during my mountain climbing experiences was James 1:12 because it said, "Blessed is the man who remains steadfast under trial, for when he has stood the test he will receive the crown of life, which God has promised to those who love him."

The reason I loved it so much is because many people falter when they are under a trial on that mountain. Many people can't handle the uncertainty of not being at their desired place on the mountain within a certain time frame. The not knowing if or when they will ever get there causes people to stumble. But those who remain mentally focused on the task at hand, and just keep taking one step at a time, can achieve whatever they set their mind to. This doesn't just apply to the big career and family goals either. This mental focus and determination helped me get through many grueling workouts. Times when I was tired and didn't think I could finish running thirty-two 100-yard sprints, I thought, *One step at a time Moats*. Times when I felt overwhelmed with homework assignments in my master's program while trying to be a great husband, father, and professional football player I thought, *One step at a time Moats*.

That mind-set is what I found necessary to continue pressing toward my goals, and through firsthand experience, I know it works. If you can embrace the adversity of climbing the mountain, the feeling of perseverance and accomplishment you will experience when you reach that mountaintop will be like no other! But if you quit and decide to turn back, you will never reach your full potential and experience the amazing things that wait for those who dare to be different!

Now, as I continue to transition through life, I'm able to lean on this experience. When I'm faced with difficult, potentially life-altering decisions, I don't allow fear to stop me from going after what I'm truly passionate about. Anytime I'm faced with a fear, I turn it into focus! Focus on being my best self! Focus on improving in some aspect every day! Focus on making the necessary sacrifices to accomplish the goal that I have set. I don't focus on being good but on being GREAT!

The mountain of fear WILL move. Choose to stand up and face it. Choose to BELIEVE in who you were created to be. Your fullest potential can be realized, but only if you learn how to put fear under your feet and focus on not just being alive but LIVING!

I have learned over the years that when one's mind is made up, this diminishes fear; knowing what must be done does away with fear.

—Rosa Parks

CHAPTER

Smile

SPREAD MY INNER LOVE
EVERYWHERE

Peace begins with a smile.

—Mother Teresa

THE POWER OF A SMILE

Did you know there is a hidden power in smiling? A smile can change the atmosphere in the whole room. A smile can turn around some-one's day. It can lengthen your life, and it can even predict a happy marriage. *Say what?!* Even forced smiles can still have an impact on the smiler and the recipient.

Have you ever had a rough day and just weren't feeling in the mood to be around people? But then someone smiled at you, and you couldn't help but start feeling better? Or what about that automatic response when someone smiles at you, and you can't help but smile back? It's the power of love expressed through a smile.

A smile is hard to resist. It doesn't matter who we are, where in the world we live, or what kind of day we're having. Smiling brings our love to the surface.

Smiling is a kindness to those who need encouragement. A smile is a peace offering when you first meet someone. A smile can change the atmosphere of the room, A genuine smile can melt the hardest of hearts. Think of the impact you can have on someone who is in a rough situation or not feeling their best, just by smiling at them.

Smiling at someone elicits a reaction from them. Nine times out of ten, they are going to smile back at you. When I smile at people, and they smile back, I'm able to help release the endorphins in that person and ultimately make them feel better. In a way, I am leaving them in a better place than when I first came into contact with them.

A smile is priceless when you think about what it costs you, but the impact it has on people is so rewarding. It's more than expressing happiness. A smile releases our inner love. It connects another person with your inner happiness, your inner joy, your inner peace, and most importantly, your inner love.

When you smile, all of those feelings are being combined and brought to the surface. A smile is like a three-dimensional emotional release of your inner love meant to make someone feel better.

TWO THOUSAND CHOCOLATE BARS

There have been studies done on the effect of smiling on life spans. In 2010, researchers studied the life span of Major League Baseball players before the 1950s.[1] They studied those who smiled and those who did not smile on their baseball cards. "The researchers found that the span of a player's smile could actually predict the span of his life. Players who didn't smile in their pictures lived an average of only 72.9 years, where players with beaming smiles lived an average of almost 80 years." *Whoa! An extra seven years on your life if you smile? Now I've got your attention!*

According to a UC Berkley 30-year study,[2] researchers were able to predict how successful people would be by using photographs of them from yearbooks. They studied those who smiled and those who didn't. The smilers had more fulfilling and long-lasting marriages, scored higher on standardized tests of well-being and happiness, and were more inspiring to others. To top it all off, the wider the smile in the photographs, the more successful they were.

In a neuroscience study on smiling in the United Kingdom, they found that one smile gave the same brain stimulation that 2,000 chocolate bars would give.[3] Not only that, but a smile could stimulate the brain just as much as receiving $25,000. *Now I want some of that kind of happiness!*

This is what we do when we smile, and that's why it feels so good to smile at someone and why it feels so good to have someone smile at you. It's the equivalent of eating 2,000 chocolate bars. *Or maybe I'll take the $25,000 option!*

Why shouldn't we try to smile more if it doesn't cost us anything and the potential return on that smile is improving the overall mood of someone? That's the equivalent of me telling you if you invest $0 with me the return on that money will be $25,000. You would already be committed to that before I could even finish my sentence, so why not take that same approach when it comes to improving the quality of life, not only for ourselves but of those around us as well? I believe we all want to genuinely be happy, and we all want this world to improve, so why not start with the person in the mirror? Why not start being the change we want to see in this world and ultimately making a difference so that the world we leave behind for our children is drastically better than the world we are currently experiencing?

A PERSONAL TEST

Most of us associate smiling with strictly the good times, spreading love when life is positive and easy. Smiling is easy when everything is going well. But as Dr. Martin Luther King Jr. said, "The ultimate measure of a man is not where he stands in moments of comfort and convenience, but where he stands at times of challenge and controversy."

One of the more challenging situations that I went through with my wife early on was the difficulty of managing a blended family. Having more than two parents involved in decision making is tough. We needed to relocate, and we could not come to a consensus. Everyone had an opinion, and it was easy to get discouraged. But at the same time, even though I would get discouraged, I would decide to put a smile on and give strength to my family by spreading my inner love. I tried to keep the stress of the situation to a minimum, and we tried to keep the negativity down by keeping our love on. We were keeping our smile on even during the tough parts of the relationship.

Now I don't mean we were pretending like we weren't under stress. I mean, we kept a positive outlook that everything was going to turn out okay. Smiles can turn tears into reassurance. Even if things don't go our way, even though we're not satisfied, we're able to smile through it. It's going to be okay. Let's keep our inner love at the forefront.

When we go through trials in the situation of being in a blended family, and when lifestyles and family dynamics begin to clash, smiling can release the tension. And then you can see a little more clearly to resolve the conflict. Even with someone who may seem like an enemy, keeping a positive attitude and keeping your smile on is going to help the situation a lot more than letting them get under your skin.

My favorite movie as a child was *The Lion King*. When I smile in the face of adversity, I feel like the young lion Simba who said, "I laugh in the face of danger." We have to see the uncomfortable things in our lives and keep our smiles on. Sometimes it will keep you from making big mistakes. Smiling and keeping a positive attitude will keep you from fight or flight. It will keep you from crumbling under tough situations. Keeping the faith that it's all going to turn out is key to not getting stuck in the conflict.

A positive outlook will always help to keep a situation healthier. I hate to use the old cliché of the glass half full, but in this case, it's true. I'm always hopeful in my thought process because negativity is going to breed negativity. If I believe the relationships in our blended family are simply not going to work, then they probably aren't. If I have a pessimistic outlook and become offended by the situation, I ruin the chances of finding the best solution for everyone.

It's easy to be angry. It's easy to cry. It's easy to be discouraged. But if you take the initial step of smiling and have a positive mental focus that everything will turn out in the end, you can save yourself a lot of angst.

Smiling is a way of recalibrating yourself and others. It's a way of starting with a fresh perspective.

RECEIVING LOVE

As I talk about the SMILE aspect of my theory of life, I recognize and understand that some of us may not have a full tank of love to draw from. It's hard to give love if you aren't receiving love.

Giving and receiving love is the foundation for a healthy life. There have been seasons in my own life when I wasn't receiving love because I had my walls up. Back when I was not open with my wife, I was dying for someone to love me, but my pride had to protect me from being vulnerable. The fear of being exposed as a weak person out-weighed my desire to be loved. *Now that's some messed up thinking!*

When I took my walls of insecurity down, there were places in my soul that began receiving much-needed love. My wife didn't reject me because of my flaws, she embraced them and brought health to my flaws with her love. The one thing I needed to become a whole person was love, but my pride kept me from receiving that love.

Trauma and pain can also keep us from getting the healing medi-cine of love to the places that need it most. When we've been rejected by those closest to us, we fear getting hurt again. We build walls and wear masks, and love can't get where it needs to go. The river of love that could reach our deepest pains is cut off by bitterness, fear, and self-protection.

The love we lacked as a child becomes our greatest need as an adult. If our parents neglected us, we are in deep need of a con-nection in adulthood. If we were bullied and rejected as a child, we have a deep need to belong to a tribe when we get older. If we never heard words of affirmation growing up, words mean so much more to us as adults. Whether good or bad, words have more meaning to those who lacked hearing positivity growing up.

The research that Dr. Gary Chapman has done on the five love languages is truly an important concept to look at.[4] Dr. Chapman surmises, after years of marriage and family counseling, that there are five emotional love languages. There are five ways that people give and receive emotional love.

Words of affirmation express love through words. Compliments or words of appreciation have a high level of effectiveness for people who need this kind of love. This is not true of everyone. Not everyone uses this kind of fuel in their "love tank," as Dr. Chapman describes it.

Quality time is when we show love by giving someone our undivided attention. This is when someone shows you how important you are by shutting off their phones and connecting person to person. Spending time with someone who uses this kind of love fuel is a powerful way to fill their tank.

Receiving gifts can be a love language to someone. When you bring home a gift, it fills this person's love tank to think that they were on your mind while you were out. Being remembered is the fuel this person needs.

Acts of service is when you fill someone's love tank by serving them. Expressing love by doing chores, planning a dinner, picking up the kids, or helping a friend with their yard are all examples of acts of service. *I bet ya'll have already guessed this one is me!*

The final love language in Dr. Chapman's research is physical touch. Not receiving physical love as a child creates a deficit in one's love tank. Being held and stroked and kissed are all ways that we express love to our children. People who have the love language of physical touch can get their love tank filled with a genuine hug, a brief kiss from their spouse, or even a child crawling up in their lap to snuggle.

Do one of these love languages speak to you? Do you recognize that one of them fills your love tank more than another? Is there a possibility that you have a wall up and are not receiving one of these kinds of love?

We have to be able to receive love before we can give it. Our love tank needs to be full before we start pouring it out on others. Understanding what we lacked as a child can point to our deficits as adults.

Also, if we can open our hearts to see what kind of love our own family members need, we will be creating a much more emotionally healthy family. Paying attention to which one of these love languages fills the heart of my wife is a huge step forward in the health of our marriage. Learning which language my children respond to the best will create a lifetime of healthy self-esteem and self-perception. Then, as a family, if we keep our love tanks filled, we've got enough to spread to those we serve.

Love is a fuel. We need to give and receive it as such.

SEEDS OF LOVE

We live in an angry and hurting world. So many brokenhearted and traumatized people cross our paths every day. Single parent homes are at an all-time high. The division and hatred that is separating us from one another is so discouraging. Opioids and illegal drugs use are increasing at a staggering rate.

It's like we've forgotten how to give and receive love. We've become hardened in this new age of cruelty. Since I am a man of positivity with my glass half full, I've gotta say that we need to believe we can turn it around. We've gotta be willing and begin to spread our inner love like seeds in the world.

It makes me think of that song immortalized by Dionne Warwick, "What the world needs now, is love, sweet love."

Everywhere I go, I try to spread my inner love. I smile at the clerk at the grocery checkout line. I have a real conversation with the server at the restaurant. I make sure these people know that I see them. The people I work with need to know that I genuinely care about their lives. I want to be authentic with my optimism. This is what spreading seeds of love looks like.

I have to believe that sowing love wherever I go creates a ripple effect, especially because I'm not giving my love to get anything back. It's my goal just to make people feel good about themselves. It's my hope that someone feels valued because I purposely deposited a seed in their day.

What if we could gather an army of seed sowers? What if we could consciously come together and be an Army of Love? Wouldn't it be amazing to have a few thousand people in every city who intentionally sowed seeds of love when they left their home? An Army of Love that was ready at any moment to say something nice or give a genuine compliment to a stranger would be an incredible force for good. Intentional positivity, intentional encouragement, intentional seed sowers. What might that look like?

I'll tell you: That looks to me like the start of a revolution. Love always wins. In the midst of darkness, the light wins.

I know I already quoted him once in this chapter, but Martin Luther King Jr. is the man when it comes to love. He said it this way, "Darkness cannot drive out darkness; only light can do that. Hate cannot drive out hate; only love can do that."

So, let's put it into practice. Let's start a crusade of intentional love. Are you ready to be a light in the darkness? Will you consider joining my Army of Love? Will you consider smiling at a stranger who looks like they need encouragement? Will you compliment your coworkers and the people who serve you in your community? Will you give a little more grace to the driver who cut you off on the interstate? What would happen if we intentionally spread seeds of love?

I say we try it and find out! Start spreading your inner love and let God take it from there.

A warm smile is the universal language of kindness.
—William Arthur Ward

Conclusion

End Zone

The only place success comes before work is in the dictionary.
—Vince Lombardi

VALLEYS AND MOUNTAINS

So many people want to be successful, but they don't want to pay the price to be successful. Many people are desperate for their dreams to come true, but they are unwilling to do what it takes to make their dreams happen. They want what's at the top of the mountain, but they are unwilling to go through the valley that eventually leads to the mountain.

Men who dream about playing football want to be the star out there on the field. They want the glamour of Sundays. They want to be loved by the fans and recognized when they go places. They want people to ask for autographs. They want to be seen as a star or a celebrity. But they don't want to be a professional.

There's a difference between being a professional and being a star. A professional puts the work in. They put countless hours in at the gym. They make sacrifices. They accept the pain and soreness. You can't just be a star. You've got to be a professional.

People want to be happy. They want the perfect life. They want to have a successful life, but they don't want to do what it takes. There is a necessary humbling that has to take place, or the dream won't last. There is a vulnerability that is learned in the valley, and it is a necessary skill you learn in order to climb the mountain.

You can't enjoy the fruits without labor. You can't enjoy the mountain without going through the valley. They don't want to make these sacrifices, they don't want to humble themselves, they don't want to have to show that vulnerability. And you can't have one without the other. You can't enjoy the fruits without that labor. The mountain tops are hollow without the valley. It's an empty success.

As you face the valleys and mountains, you begin to understand that life is full of them. Every mountain is followed by a valley. And every valley is followed by a mountain.

It's important that you enjoy that mountain climb. It's important to learn in the valley. As long as we keep pressing forward, there's another mountain that's waiting on you to conquer. There's another valley to grow through.

But this is where one of my favorite scriptures comes into focus. I just love Psalm 23.

Psalm 23[1]
The Lord is my shepherd, I lack nothing.
He makes me lie down in green pastures,
he leads me beside quiet waters,
he refreshes my soul.

He guides me along the right paths for his name's sake.
Even though I walk through the darkest valley,
I will fear no evil, for you are with me;
your rod and your staff, they comfort me.

You prepare a table before me in the presence of my enemies.
You anoint my head with oil; my cup overflows.

Surely your goodness and love will follow me
all the days of my life,
and I will dwell in the house of the Lord forever.

You are never going to be alone while you're going through the mountains and the valleys. You're always going to be able to handle what comes your way because God is with you, so just keep going with it.

Don't stop in the valley.

There is an ebb and flow of life. If you want to get to the mountain, you've got to go through the valley. Embrace it. Embrace the valley experience, because you know it's going to lead to something awesome once you get through it.

Not all valleys are going to be the same. Some valleys will be short, and others will be forty days and forty nights. But there's a reason for it. It's a part of the process. Embrace the process in the valleys and don't say, "I hate the valleys." Because if you hate the process and resist the changes that need to happen, you're never going to get to that mountaintop. Turn your fear into focus. Smile through it. Look to inspire others along the way. You see how this theory of mine is starting to play out?

King David went through the valley, and he learned from it. He gained wisdom, understanding, and skills through his lonely seasons and his cave experience.

David was acquainted with valleys and mountains. As a teenager, he was in the field, rejected by his family, not understanding that he was learning to fight giants. The lessons he learned in his lonely time in the field led him to a mountaintop experience of bringing down Goliath. He came back from the fight with a sword in one hand and the giant's head in the other. *That's a mountaintop!*

David found himself in another valley when he stumbled by committing adultery with Bathsheba. His error caused him to have to walk through the valley again. He still had something to learn. He tried to fix it himself, which led to murder and a stain on his kingship. But he finally humbled himself before God. He went back to his faith. He remembered the cave experience. David remembered who put him on the throne in the first place. And after the valley, God led him back to the mountaintop. It's the process of life.

Some of my processing came during college football. I led my team in sacks, and I was one of the best players from a defensive standpoint, but I was facing a guy who was playing opposite me, who had more recognition because of his name. I had better stats. I was an all-around better player. But there was a lack of respect for my abilities.

I could have been hurt by it or discouraged by it, but I gotta stick with being me. I stayed on the path that was set for me, and I did not let a negative valley like that swallow me up. If I get offended at what I perceive as injustice or I fall into self-pity, it stops the lessons that need to be learned in the valley.

Some valleys seem harder or longer than the ones that others travel. But if we start comparing our paths with others, we'll stop moving through life because we got distracted and didn't focus on our own path. In my case, I kept my head down, and I kept focusing on my own path. At the end of this valley, I was awarded the Buck Buchanan FCS Award for National Defensive Player of the Year. *We call that a mountaintop baby!*

Persevere through the valleys. Smile through your low points because you know that there's a reward if you don't quit.

FAILURE ISN'T FOREVER

How many people fall and they feel embarrassed and too ashamed to admit it? They don't know how to get up, brush themselves off, and get back to work. It's unfortunate, but a lot of people feel that once they fail, it's over. I wish I could show them that failure is a bump in the road on the way to success. Everyone fails. Everyone falls off the horse once in a while.

You have to go through some failures in order to reach success, and then once you reach success, it doesn't stop there. You continually improve yourself.

I decided I wanted to go ahead and get my master's degree while playing in the NFL. I was already successful. I had my bachelor's degree. I had played in the NFL for three seasons. I was going into my fourth. This meant I had reached the point in the NFL where I would be fully invested in the NFL's player benefits program. I was now eligible for health insurance for my family when I retired. It also came with a plethora of other financial bonuses that I would acquire from my time of retirement up until the age of 65. That was a big thing for me. It was during this time I decided that I wanted to push myself further. I wanted to get a master's degree while playing and being a husband and a father.

I was not satisfied with just being successful on the football field. I wanted to continue to be my best self. Even though it took me three years instead of two to complete, I still accomplished it while being a husband, while having three kids, and while still being a successful NFL player. It's important to press forward and not rest on your successes. It's important to improve your life regardless of where you are in life. It doesn't matter if you're a sixteen-year-old in high school, or you're a sixty-year-old CEO. You are never going to peak. The only time you peak is when you're dead.

That's how I look at it. I never want to believe that something can't get any better. There's always room for improvement in your marriage, as a father, in your career, or simply being a man. Complacency is the beginning of the end.

How many times have I heard Coach Tomlin say, "More grounded, more humble, more selfless." That's a great quote. And one that will be true in all stages of life.

I try not to lose sight of those words. But the truth is, some guys don't want to be humbled. They don't want to have to be vulnerable. They don't want to go through the process. But there's a price to pay for not humbling yourself. Humility is what makes success last.

When you humble yourself, you learn that success is not all about you. You learn that worldly success can come and go, but it doesn't change your value. This is something that can only be achieved through humility. And humility is learned in the valleys. Being grounded, selfless, and humble sets you up to be ready for the next opportunity. It prepares you for the next Goliath. It gives you the wisdom to climb the next mountain.

Humility causes you to recognize that success is more than football stats.

Another one of Coach Tomlin's sayings is, "It's not what you're capable of, it's what you're willing to do."

How many people are capable of great things? You might feel that you're capable of being the president of the United States, but are you willing to do what's necessary to get there? What are you willing to give up to reach that? What kind of process are you willing to go through to make that possible?

You might be capable, but are you willing?

Everyone is capable of being a success. We all have gifts that are very specific to each of us, but what are you willing to give up to watch them grow? Are you willing to put the work in, to make sure the soil's good? What's your character like? Is it where it needs to be? Are you tending to your gifts? Are you making sure that your heart is getting the sunlight that it needs? Success is reached through the careful tending of our hearts, gifts, and character. Plenty of people want success, but they don't want to do everything that leads to it. And something we all need to ask ourselves is, Do I have the correct definition of success? Because success for the accolades is empty.

M.O.A.T.S. THEORY OF LIFE

I want to take you back to one of the first points I made in Chapter M. We discussed making happiness a priority. Now that we have meandered through the points that inspire me and the points that I try to inspire others with, let's revisit why your happiness is important.

When we reach success without finding our *why*, we're hollow on the inside. But if we do the thing we were put on the earth to do, we find fulfillment. We make happiness a priority by understanding that success in and of itself is not happiness.

That's why I had to go back into my childhood and remember what it was that made me happy. I had success on the field. I had the dream house and the family I always wanted. But I wasn't happy because I wasn't doing what I had been put here to do. Chasing after the applause of men was not success. Getting drafted in the NFL wasn't enough. Having a family and a home wasn't enough. I could have even been an MVP, or a Superbowl champ, I could have owned a Fortune 500 company, but none of it would have made me happy. Because my purpose is to inspire and impact others to become everything they were created to be.

You need to search your own heart and pray to know why you were put on the earth. Because when you know it and when you do it, you'll find happiness.

When I found what made me happy, it put a spotlight on my identity. Because I *had* been doing community outreach, but I never viewed that as the focal point. I saw it wrong. I viewed my success as doing well at football or getting good grades in school. I wrongly measured success by how many people loved me.

I had to look deeper into what I was lacking, I had to face the hollow feeling and admit that something wasn't quite right. I felt terrible that the success I longed to have now seemed so empty.

But when I realized that my *why* was positively impacting the lives of others, it brought my life into focus. I didn't know I was out of focus until I faced the hollowness of worldly success.

I needed to remove the warped glasses from my eyes. It caused me to see a warped reality. It was right before me the whole time, but I couldn't see it until the incorrect lenses were removed. I see more clearly now. I can see things that make me a better man. I can see things that make me happy. I can focus in a new way, and going forward I know where my focus is and where my priorities are.

Not everybody's happiness is going to look exactly the same. Not everyone is called to have the servant's heart that I have. Some people are called to be vocal and lead. Others are called to build businesses. Some are called to write. Still, others are called to pour into kids. There are so many possibilities.

I desire to spur you on to find what you are on this earth to do. What is your *why*? And who is it for? What is it that shines a light on your identity?

Maybe you already know what it is. Maybe you are already doing it. I am so happy for you! I hope that my words have encouraged you somehow to grow in your calling. But if you aren't sure that you are doing the thing you were meant to do, I hope the story of my journey will catapult you into a season of searching for your purpose.

It's my sincere desire that my Theory of Life will somehow impact those who read it. May it inspire people to begin to live their lives to the fullest by doing what makes them happy. May my words encourage people to have open and authentic relationships with those who are closest to them. I want to challenge my readers to become an army of inspirers. I want them to light the fire of inspiration in the souls of those who are on the journey with them. I hope that my words strengthen the hearts of people who have Goliaths to kill and mountains to climb.

And finally, I want to teach the world to SMILE a little more often! You can't go wrong with a smile, because you can't go wrong with love. Open up your heart and spread your inner love everywhere.

God put you here for a reason. He's with you in the valleys and the mountains. He'll never leave you or forsake you. The Bible says He wrote out every one of your days before any of them came to be. Trust in His plan. Put your hand in His and let Him lead you down the path He's made specifically for you.

"For I know the plans I have for you," declares the LORD, "plans to prosper you and not to harm you, plans to give you hope and a future."

—Jeremiah 29:11

ENDNOTES

CHAPTER 1

1. Brian Galliford, "Arthur Moats Officially Ends Brett Favre's Consecutive Games Played Streak," *Buffalo Rumblings* (blog), December 13, 2010, http://www.buffalorumblings. com/2010/12/13/1874484/arthur-moats-officially-ends-brett-favres-consecutive-games-played.

CHAPTER "S"

1. Ernest L. Abel and Michael L. Kruger, "Smile Intensity in Photographs Predicts Longevity," *Psychological Science*, 2010, https://doi.org/10.1177/0956797610363775.
2. Eric Savitz, "The Untapped Power of Smiling." *Forbes*, August 10, 2011, http://www.forbes.com/sites/ericsavitz/2011/03/22/the-untapped-power-of-smiling/#355d31c37a67.
3. Melanie Curtin, "Neuroscience Says Doing This 1 Thing Makes You Just as Happy as Eating 2,000 Chocolate Bars." *Inc.com,* August 29, 2017, http://www.inc.com/melanie-curtin/science-says-doing-this-makes-you-just-as-happy-as.html.
4. Gary D. Chapman, *The 5 Love Languages: The Secret to Love That Lasts* (Chicago: Northfield Publishing, 2010).

CONCLUSION

1. *The Holy Bible,* New International Version. Grand Rapids, MI: Zondervan, 2011.

My father and I, *1996*

1994

Youth Day at church, *1996*

My sister and I, *1994*

My father and I at my first football game, *1993*

1993

My father and I at my first football game, *1993*

1993

My father and I after church service, *1999*

Senior year of football Churchland high school, *2005*

High school graduation, *2006*

High school graduation, *2006*

My Father receiving the Meritorious Achievement Citation at Paris Island, SC, *April 1980*

My Father's Marine Unit MWCS-28, Cherry Point, NC, *March 1982*

My Father receiving a promotion to LCpl/E-3 at Camp Elmore Norfolk, Va, *November 1977*

SC 3rd Recruit Training, *March 1980*

SC 3rd Recruit Training, *March 1980*

SC 3rd Recruit Training, *March 1980*

SC 3rd Recruit Training, *March 1980*

Senior Night at James Madison University, *2009*

Receiving the 23rd Buck Buchanan Award

JMU senior year, *2009*

Receiving the 23rd Buck Buchanan Award

Graduating from JMU, *2012*

My mother, Rosalind, and father, Arthur Jr., and I receiving the 23rd Buck Buchanan Award, *2009*

NFL Scouting Combine, *2010* ©*NFL*

NFL Scouting Combine, *2010* ©*NFL*

Mother and I, NFL Draft Party Day 1, *2010*   The day Shonda and I got engaged, *April 2011*

The day I got drafted. *(cousins Stephanie, Tiffany, and April. Sister Chrissy, and best friend Marvin)*

1st day as a Buffalo Bill at Rookie Mini-Camp
©*Buffalo Bills*

1st NFL training camp, *2010* ©*Buffalo Bills*

Ed Wang and I giving out Thanksgiving meals in Buffalo, *2010* ©*Buffalo Bills*

1st ever NFL preseason game *(#45, vs the Washington Redskins)*, *2010 ©Buffalo Bills*

Rookie year during the regular season *(#52)*, *2010 ©Buffalo Bills*

My family and the family from the Red Cross Event, *2012 ©Buffalo Bills*

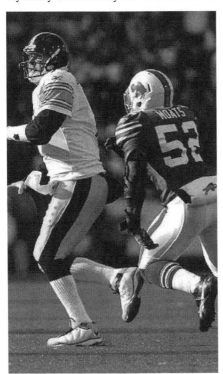

George Wilson and myself's rookie year, *2010 ©Buffalo Bills*

My rookie year vs the Steelers chasing after Ben Roethlisberger, *2010 ©Buffalo Bills*

Me hitting Brett Farve, *2010 ©Buffalo Bills*

My father and I, *2011*

Interning with the United Way Of Buffalo & Erie County, *2011*

My brother-in-law and I after a game, *2012*

My grandparents-in-law at a Bills game, *2011*

Kaylor handing out breast cancer ribbons
before a Bills home game, *2011*

Kaylor at a Bills game, *2011*

Bills game, *2011* ©*Buffalo Bills*

My mother-in-law and I, *2011*

Wedding day, *2012* ©*Jen Jar and Ashley Burnett*

Wedding day, *2012* ©*Jen Jar and Ashley Burnett*

My brother, and groomsmen "PCB Boys" before my wedding, *2012*

My grandfather, Ava, and Me, *2012*

Visiting Kaylor's Kindergarten class, *2012*

Shonda, Ava, and Kaylor at the Bills season opener, *2013*

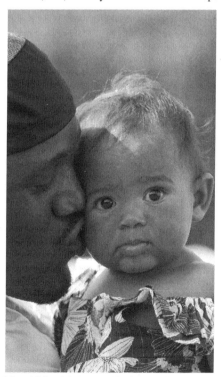

My middle girl, Ava, and I after training camp practice for the Bills, *2013*

Ava and Kaylor in the locker room, *2013*

Donating to the Buffalo School For The Performing Arts, *2013*

My "Arthur Moats Christmas Shopping Event", *2013*

My "Arthur Moats Christmas Shopping Event", *2013*

Ava and I after practice, *2013*

My sister, brother, and I after my game vs the Steelers, *2013*

Walter Payton Man Of The Year Award, *2013*

"Don't Cross The Moats", *2013*

1st start as a Steeler, *2014* ©*Pittsburgh Steelers*

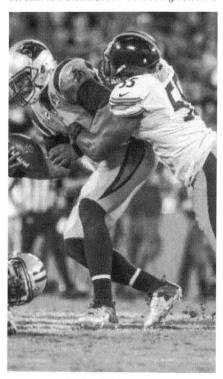

1st sack as a Steeler, *2014*
©*Pittsburgh Steelers*

Signing autographs with Ava at Steelers
training camp, *2014*

1st preseason game as a Steeler, *2014* ©*Pittsburgh Steelers*

After a Steelers home game, *2014*

Introduction, *2014* ©*Pittsburgh Steelers*

Sacking Joe Flacco of the Baltimore Ravens, *2014* ©*Pittsburgh Steelers*

Before my first Steelers home game, *2014*

Volunteering at the Ronald McDonald House Charities Of Pittsburgh "RMHC", *2015* ©*Pittsburgh Steelers*

My mother and I after a Steelers game, *2015*

All of my children together once Grey was born, *2015*

Steelers game, *2015* ©*Pittsburgh Steelers*

Coach Tomlin and I, *2015*

Steelers game, *2015* ©*Pittsburgh Steelers*

Introduction, *2015* ©*Pittsburgh Steelers*

The Trappers, *2015*

Visiting a navy seal in San Diego, California before our game vs the chargers
(With James Harrison), *2015* ©*Pittsburgh Steelers*

Family at Steelers training camp, *2015*

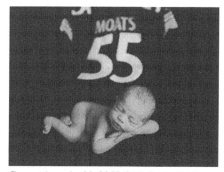

Grey at 1 week old, *2015* ©*Kimberly Carlson*

Training camp with my girls, *2015*

My children, *2015*

Postgame prayer in locker room, *2016 ©Pittsburgh Steelers*

Introduction, *2016 ©Pittsburgh Steelers*

Introduction, *2017* ©*Pittsburgh Steelers*   Grey and Me, *2017*

Grey and Me, *2017* ©*Nairobi Jones*

Arthur Moats Christmas Shopping Event, Pittsburgh, *2016* ©*Pittsburgh Steelers*

Family, *2017* ©*Nairobi Jones*

Family vacation, Bahamas, *2017*

Kaylor and I, *2017*

In the locker room, *2017*

My dog Biggie, *2017*

Training camp, *2017*

Graduation from Empire State College with my Masters Degree, *2017*

Family at Steelers Fashion Show, *2017 ©Pittsburgh Steelers*

Ava's preschool graduation, *2017*   *2017 ©Pittsburgh Steelers*

Steelers Youth Football Camp, *2018*
©Pittsburgh Steelers

My brother and me, *2017*

National Anthem *(Ben Roethlisberger, Coach Tomlin)*, *2017* *©Pittsburgh Steelers*

Working out, *2017 ©Pittsburgh Steelers*

Practice, *2017 ©Pittsburgh Steelers*

Training camp, *2017*

My father and I, *2018*

Hall of Famer Joe Greene, *2017*

Practice, *2017* ©*Pittsburgh Steelers*

Announcing Steelers 2017 NFL Draft selections, *2017 ©NFL*

Introduction, *2017 ©Pittsburgh Steelers*

Smile, AFC North Champions, *2017*

AFC North Champions, *2017* ©*Pittsburgh Steelers*

Shaking hands with Steelers President and Owner Arthur Rooney, Jr., *2017* ©*Pittsburgh Steelers*

Visiting the 911th Airlift Wing U.S. Air Force Reserve, *2017* ©*Pittsburgh Steelers*

Check presentation for Walter Payton Man Of The Year Award, *2016* ©*Pittsburgh Steelers*

Grey and I in locker room, Arizona Cardinals, *2018*

Brian the day we met "Big Brothers, Big Sisters", *2008*

Brian after his high school graduation, *2019*

Daddy Daughter Dance *(Kaylor and I)*, *2017*

Daddy Daughter Dance *(Ava and I)*, *2018*

My wife and I, *2018* ©*Hannah Hogue*

My son Grey and I, *2018* ©*Hannah Hogue*   Grey, *2018*

Shonda and I, Cayman Islands, *2018*

Family, *2018* ©*Hannah Hogue*

Family, *2018* ©*Hannah Hogue*

Made in the USA
Lexington, KY
26 November 2019